THE WALLACE FAMILY

AN ALBUM OF THE ROARING TWENTIES

A History of an American Family Living in Mid-America

From 1921 to 1930...and a little beyond

(Captured with their own camera)

By

Clarence Robert Tower

COPYRIGHT

FOREWORD

This coffee table book is a compilation of original photographs from a once discarded family album which was the proud possession of an American family living in the vicinity of the Texas - Oklahoma panhandle from 1921 to 1930 and a little beyond. It was purchased by the author in the 1960s at which time it was known to be an invaluable record of an American family's experiences during those years known as the "ROARING TWENTIES." It sat in storage until the present day to be presented as a published book.

A number of the photos contained notations on the reverse, providing documentation for time and locations where the photos were processed. Such provided the author with the information he needed to pin down the time span and the locations involved. In addition, an assortment of printed paper, including postcards and related business records came with the album to further help piece the story together.

This is no ordinary album. It contains marvelous photos of the classic automobiles of the time. It documents the family's travels from Niagara Falls and Washington D.C., to the California coast. They passed through the campus of Notre Dame University at the time it was being visited by the Goodyear Blimp and at the time the Notre Dame Football stadium was under construction. The father was a fully involved Kiwanis member – an event of which appears in the album.

At home, they swam in the local lakes and reservoirs and spread out their picnic blankets on the banks of the lakes, filmed their cars amidst the cottonfields. The father was the "Great Hunter and Fisherman." He traveled near and far to seek out his prey and bountiful catches, leaving us marvelous photos of their safari camps and trophies. The photos include a menacing mountain lion, numerous trophy deer, armadillo, huge catches of fish and dozens of wild foul. This was a family that pursued life to the fullest.

The focus of their attention was obviously the baby shown naked on the blanket. His name is noted as James R. Wallace, but nothing is written about others in the photos. By playing with numbers, the author was able to ascertain that his date of birth was most likely Dec. 21, 1921.

The fate of the family after this album is not known. For that reason, the basic format throughout will be "What must have been their thoughts and feelings – we can only guess."

PHOTO RESTORATION

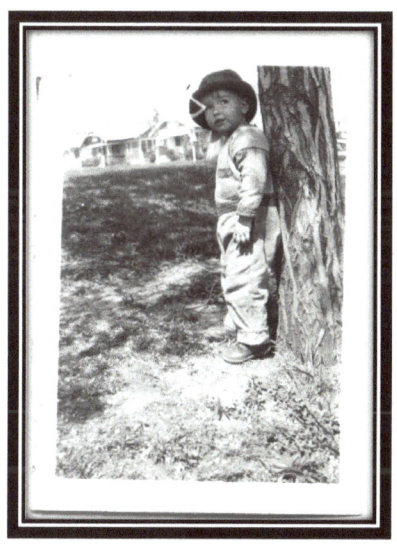 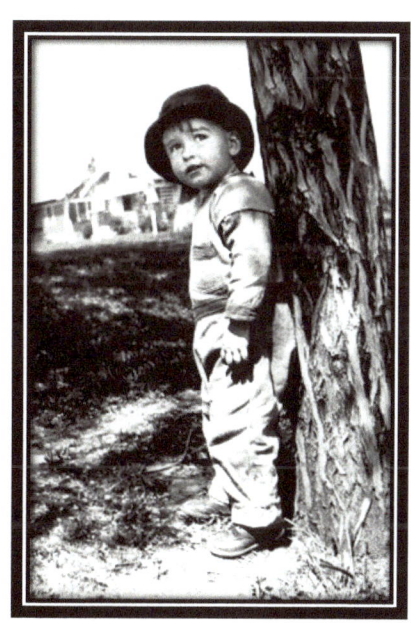

A significant amount of time was expended on photo restoration before the photos could qualify as being "book ready." The photos at left and right are good examples of "before and after." Recognizing that a majority of the hunting photos were taken with a simple box camera, a small number were too faded or damaged to be fully restored. However, they were too valuable to the storyline to be left out, so they have been included as "best restoration possible."

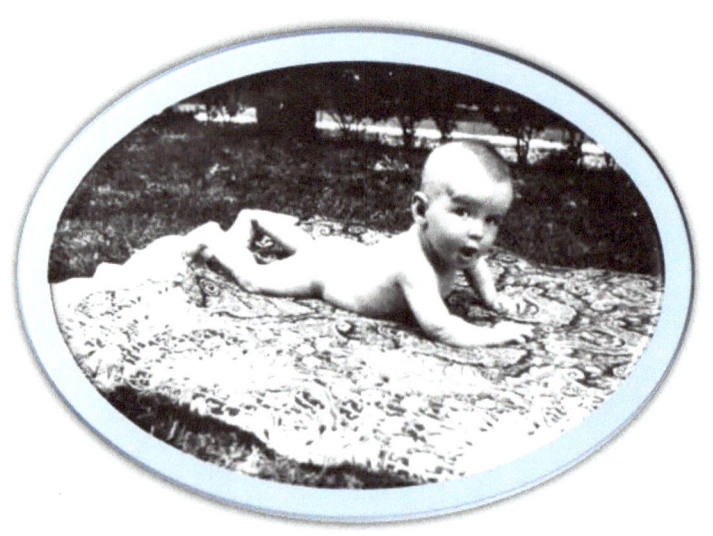

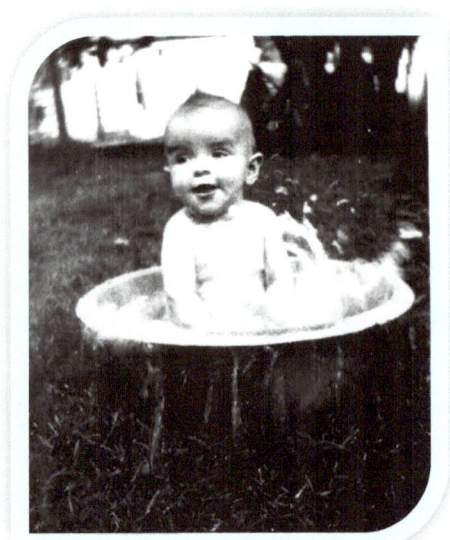

Baby J. R.

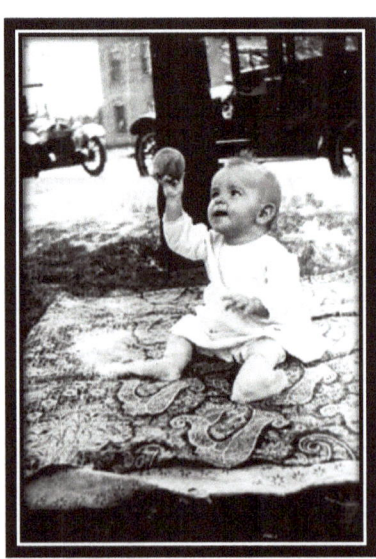

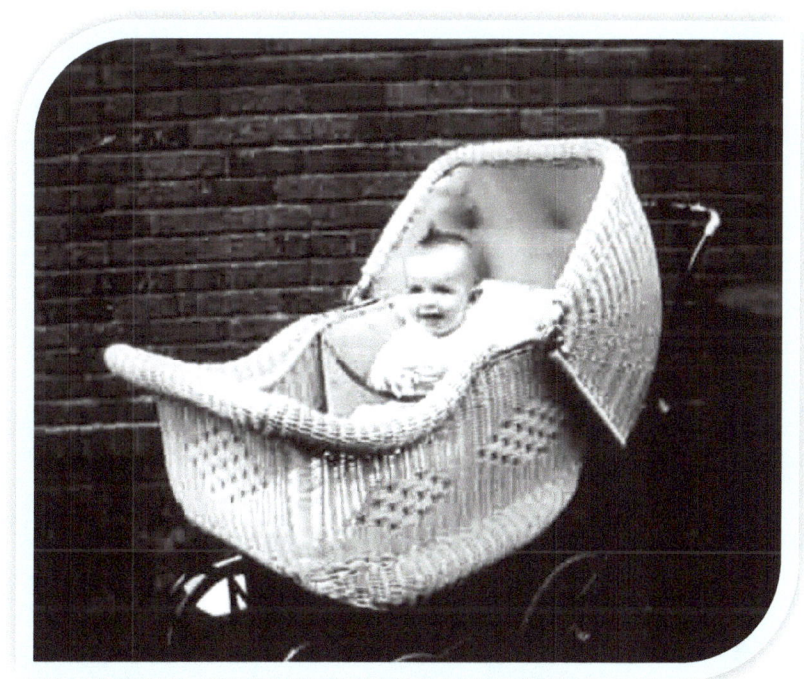

A smiling J. R.
let's everyone know he is having a good day.

As readers will see as they go through the book, nothing was spared when it came to providing the finest for J. R.

Wicker carriages, like the one shown here, were "top-of-the-line" during those years and to this day remain as highly-treasured remembrances of the 1920s era.

J. R. with Mom and Dad

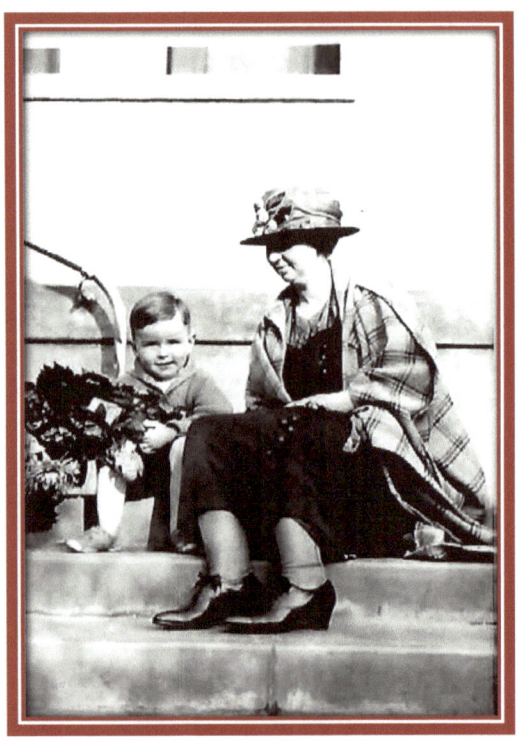 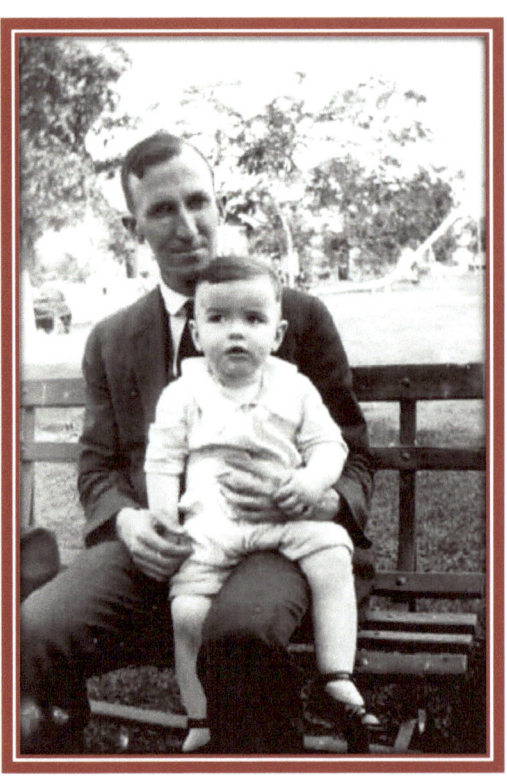

J.R. with Mom, 1920s style   *Six months old J.R. on Dad's lap*

The album contained more than 40 photographs of Mom's and Dad's only son, James R., during his toddler years

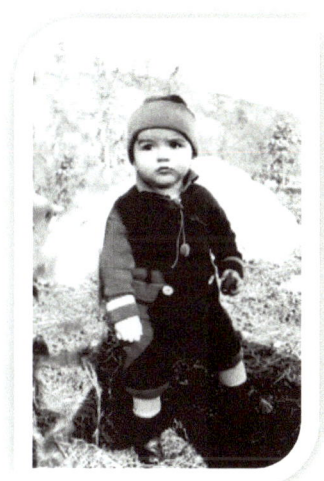
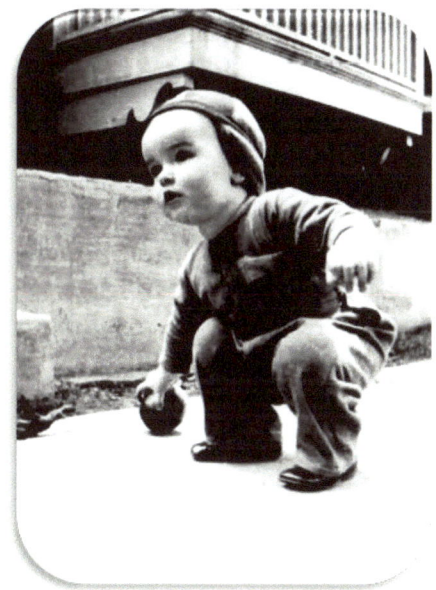
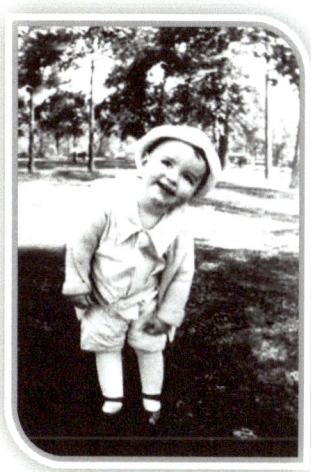

More J. R. - Always in Style

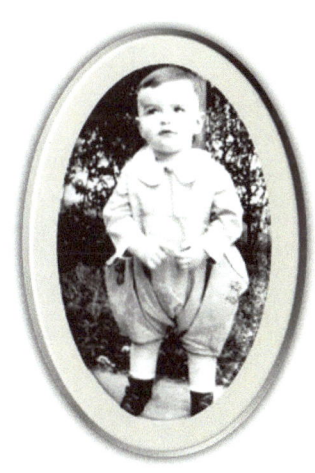
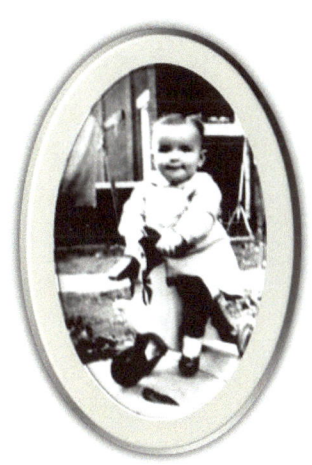

The photos on the previous page and this page span J.R.'s age of 11 months to 17 1/2 months. Nothing was spared when it came to providing the finest for J. R. The photo on previous page, bottom left was taken on Easter Sunday.

Smile for the Camera!

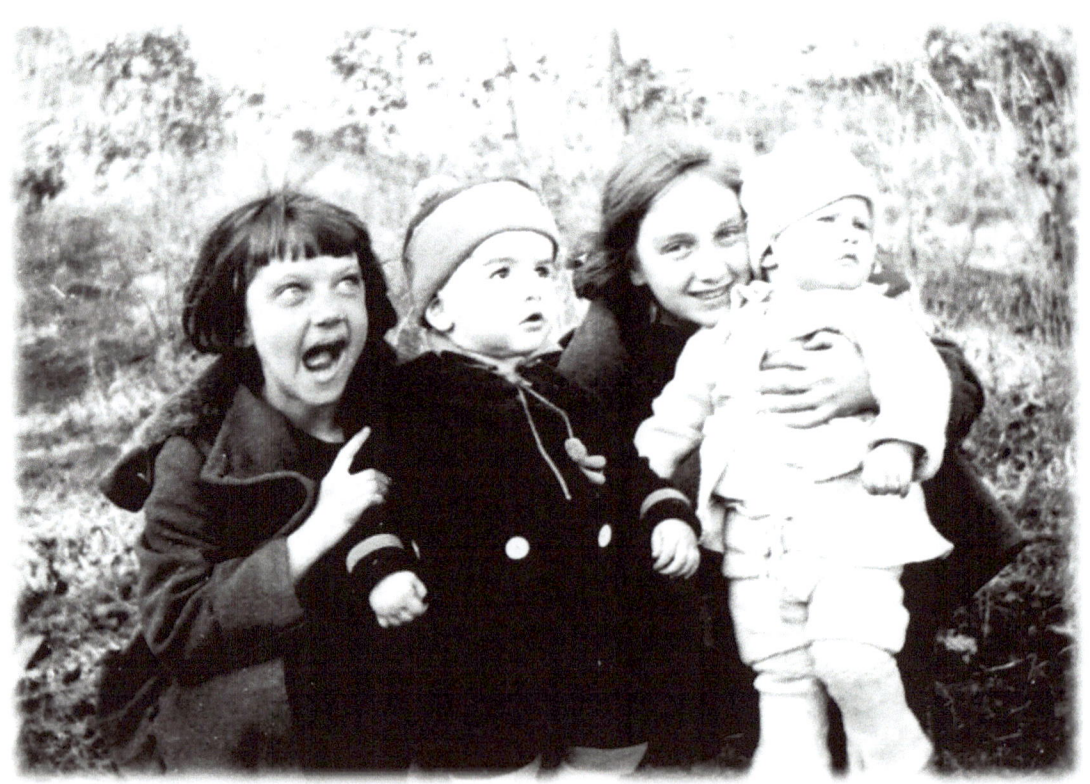

J. R. in the black coat

Country Boy all the way

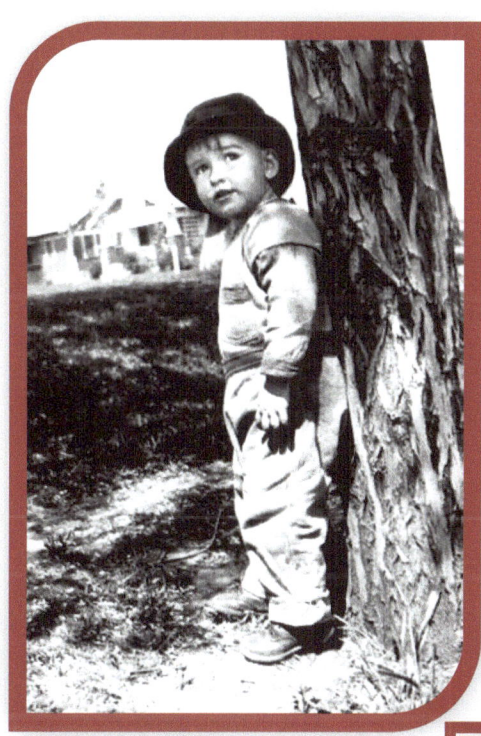

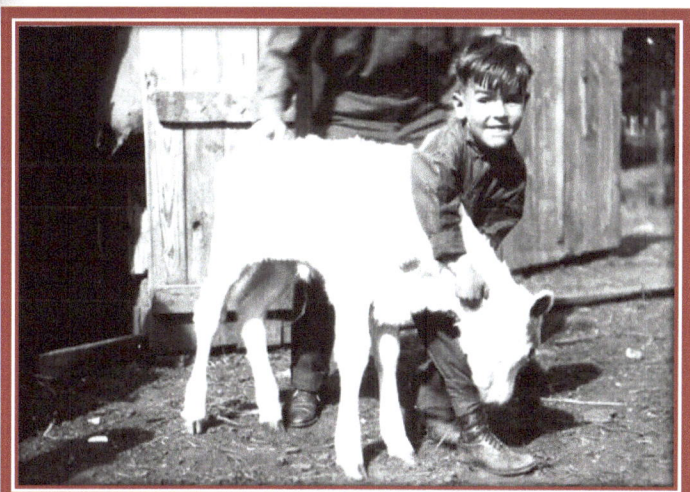

"Kid J.R." Homemade Toys Were the Thing

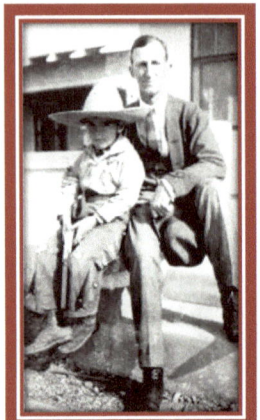

J. R. (left) is holding a handmade "RUBBER GUN" (rifle), most probably made of a factory-wood strip with pieces added for the stock.

(The author also had one during his childhood.)

The clue to why it is assumed to be a rubber gun, rather than a real gun or B.B. gun, is revealed by the photo in the lower right.

Notice the assortment of narrow strips hanging from his belt-line. These are rubber bands cut from discarded automobile inner-tubes. This was J. R.'s ammunition. One end was locked into a notch at the barrel-end. The rubber band was subsequently stretched the length of the barrel to again be locked into a trigger device. The rubber band was fired by releasing the trigger device. This is a forgotten measure of those great times.

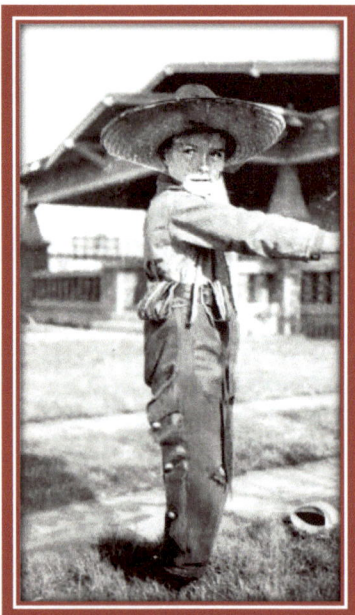

Someone visiting for sure

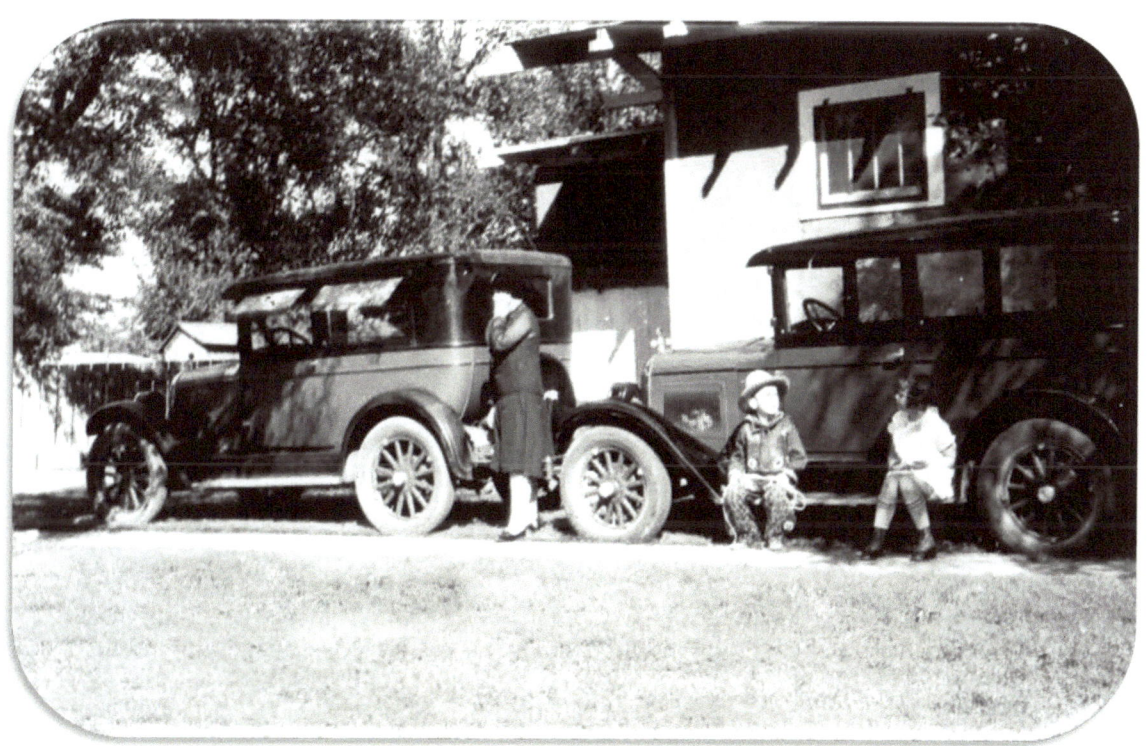

Notice the shades on the left side of the front car.

A Pose for eternity

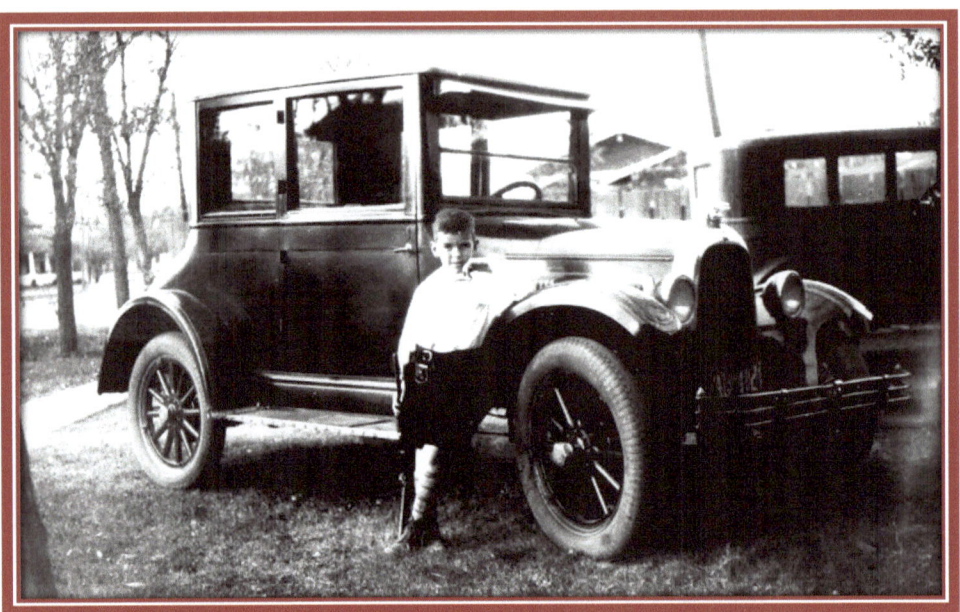

A switch from rubber guns to a B. B. gun.
(That's a Jaguar emblem on the hood of the car.)

J. R. did all the things that kids do.

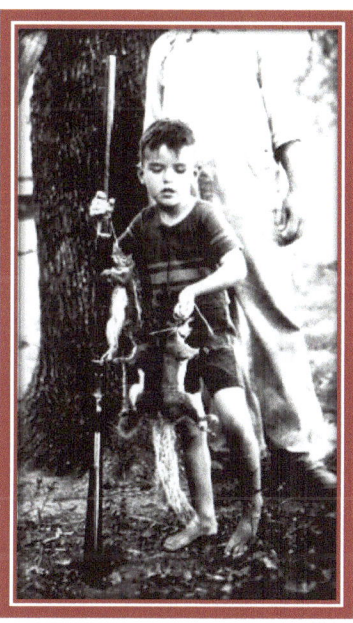 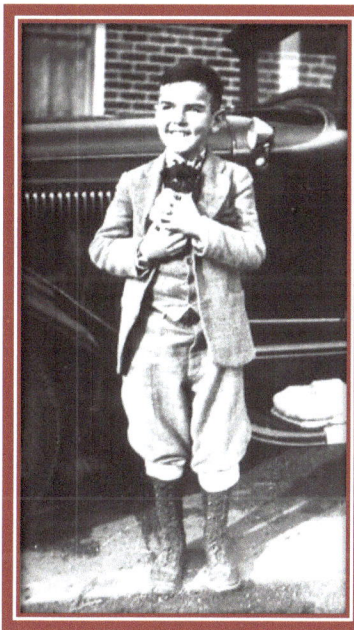 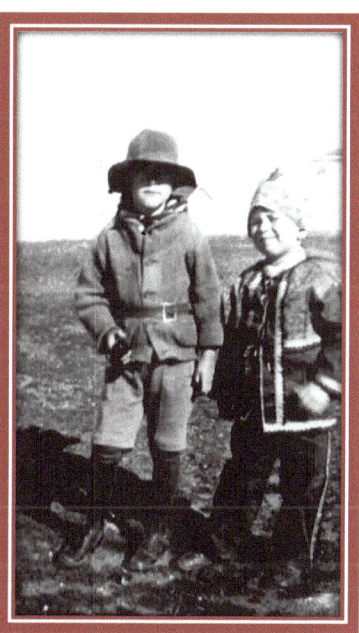

The photo at left proves that no one was concerned about letting J. R. handle a real rifle.

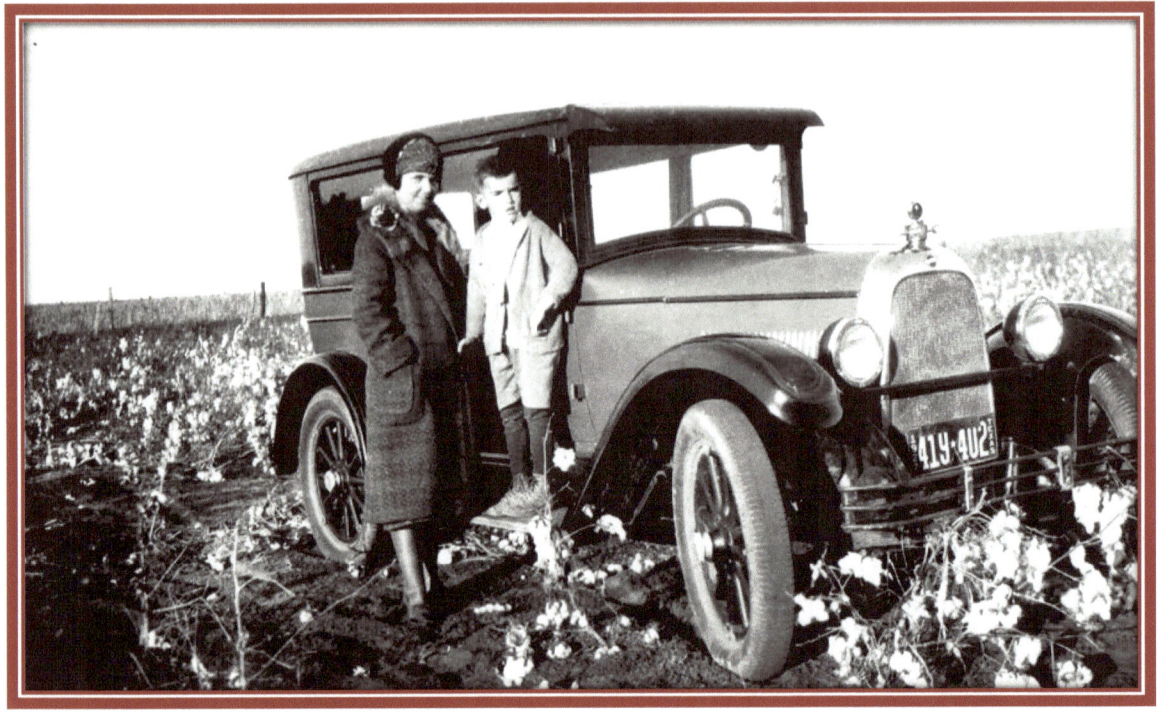

Mom and J.R. in a cottonfield

CARS...CARS...CARS!

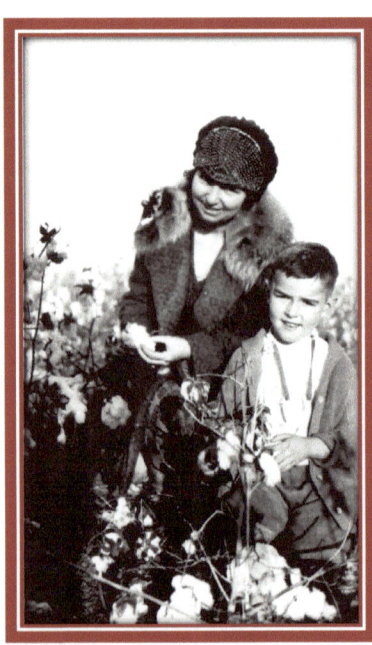

More cars-cars-cars!

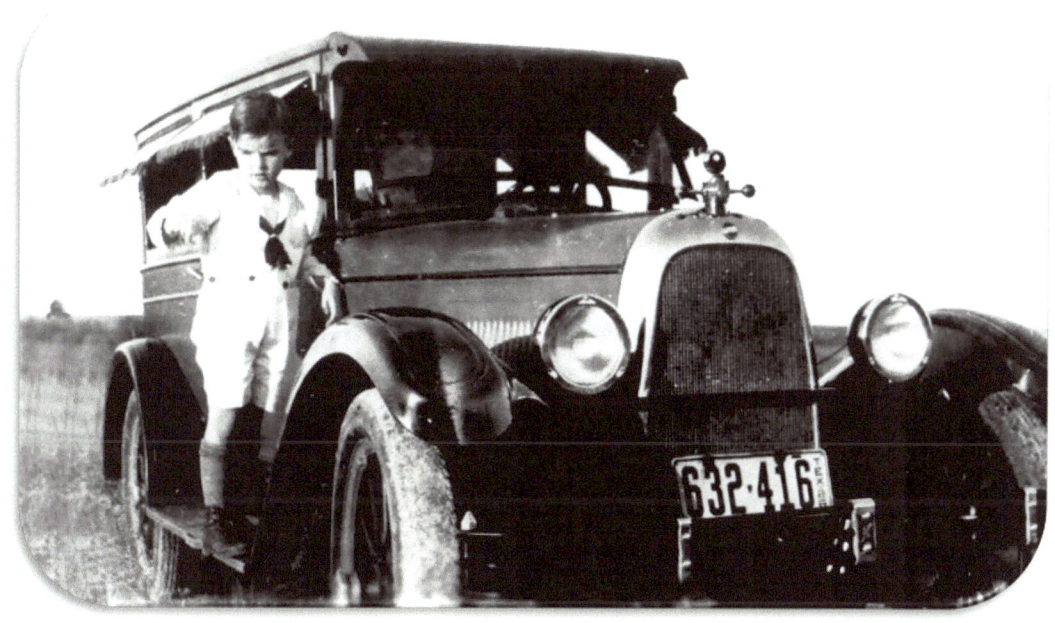

This looks the same as the car in the cotton fields, but note the different license plate. We learn later that the father owned an automobile supply business.

The neighborhood

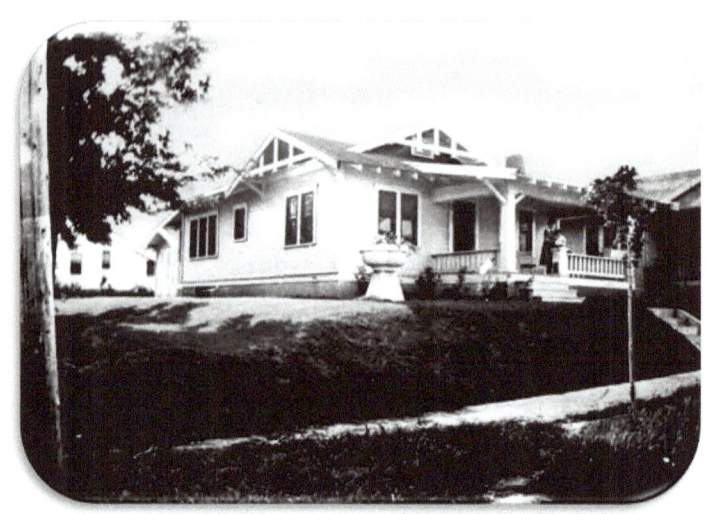

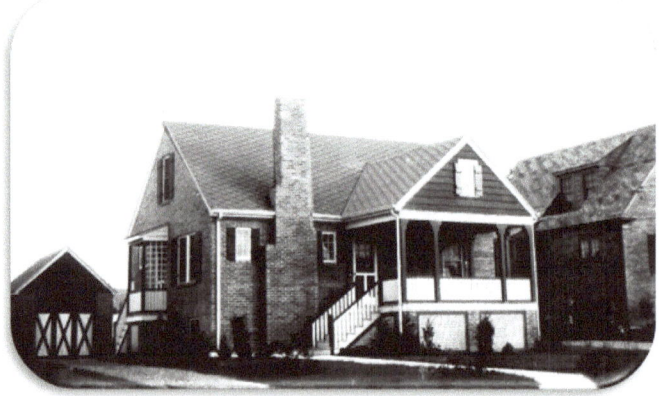

Two of the houses found in the album.

AN ALBUM OF THE ROARING TWENTIES

Friends, Neighbors or relatives – We can only guess.

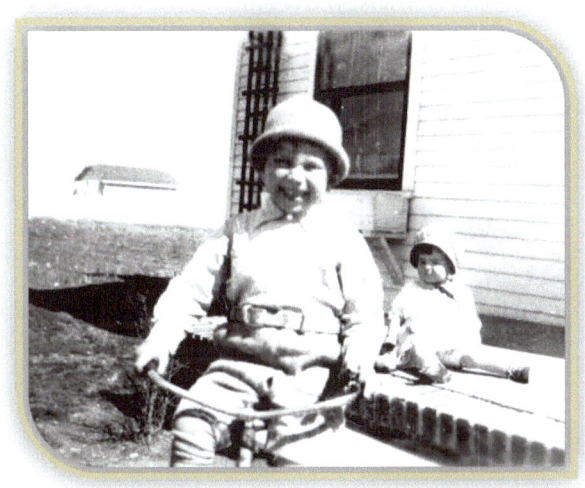

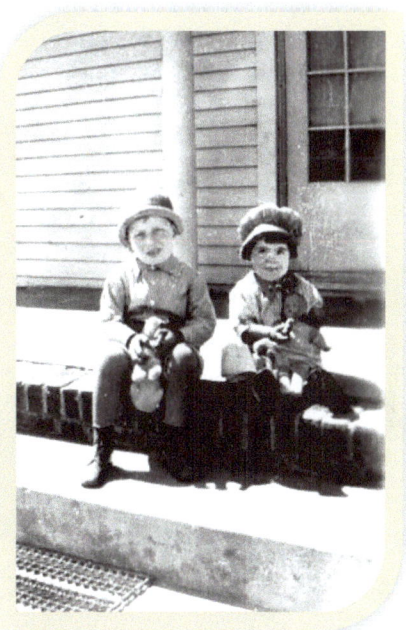

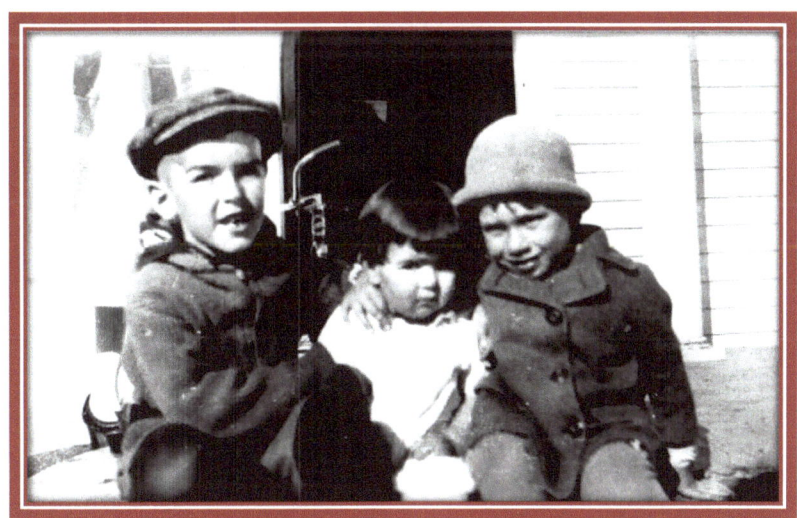

Another of the many cars possessed. Fortunately, the album captured both old and new cars of the era.

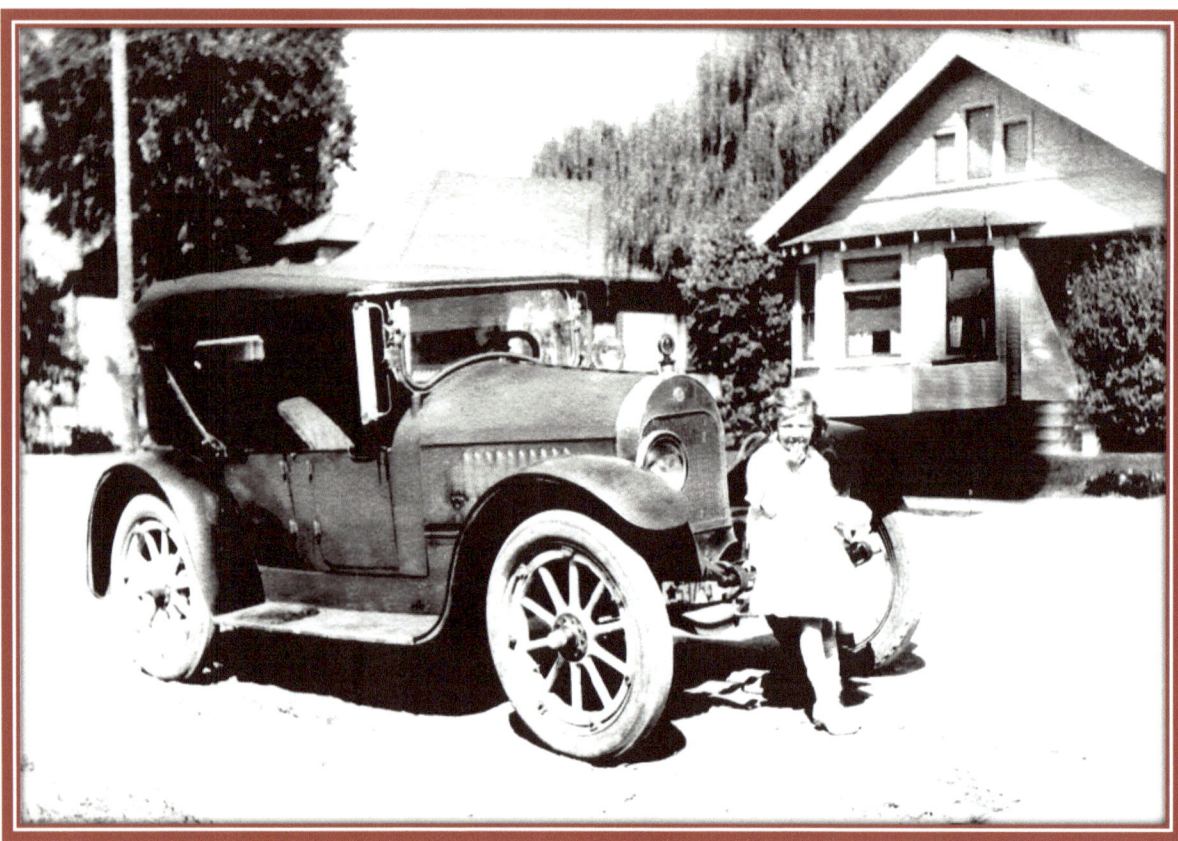

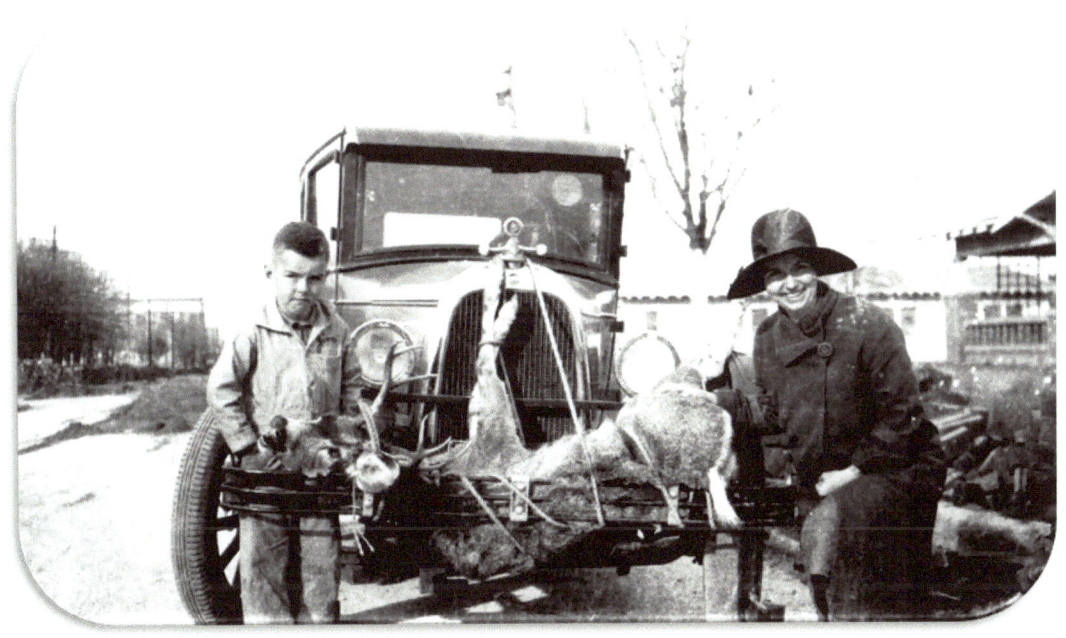

A gift to the family from the "Great Hunter"

J. R. is not too impressed at the deer on the bumper,

but Mom is immensely so.

The business car?

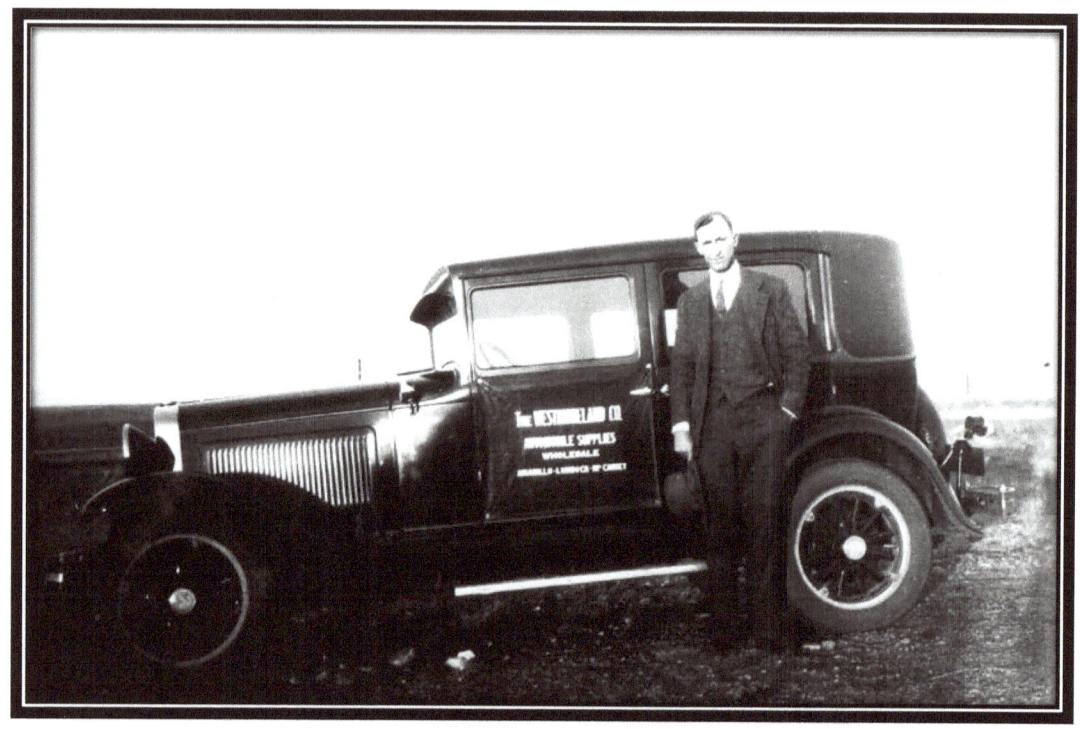

The sign on the door panel reads:

THE WESTMORELAND CO. AUTOMOBILE SUPPLIES –

WHOLESALE – AMARILLO – LUBBOCK – N CAMEY

A buddy's business?

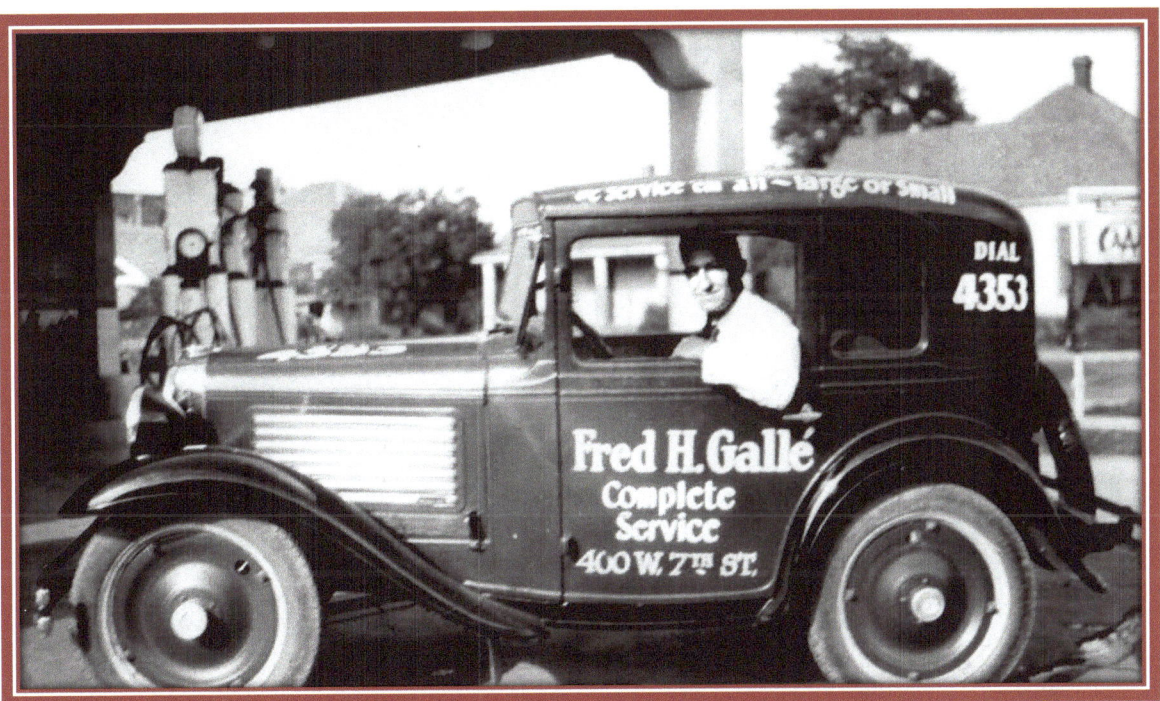

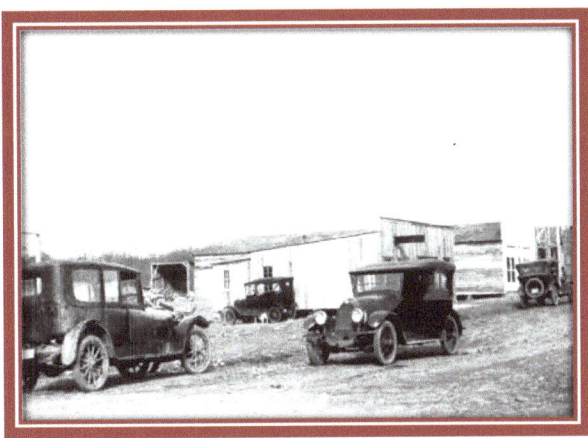

Lake Worth Texas

Buddies at the Plano7Club.

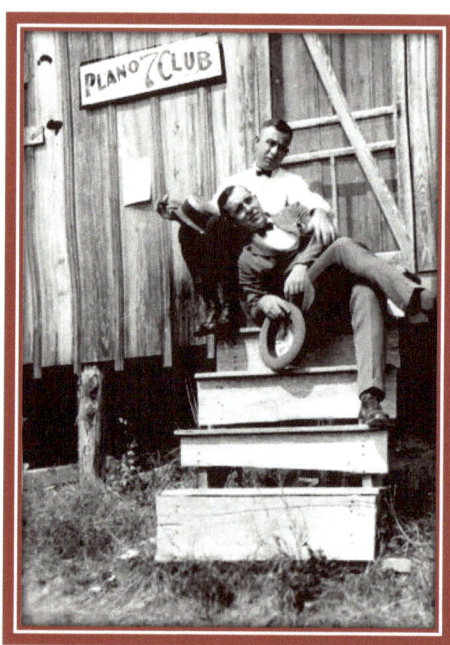

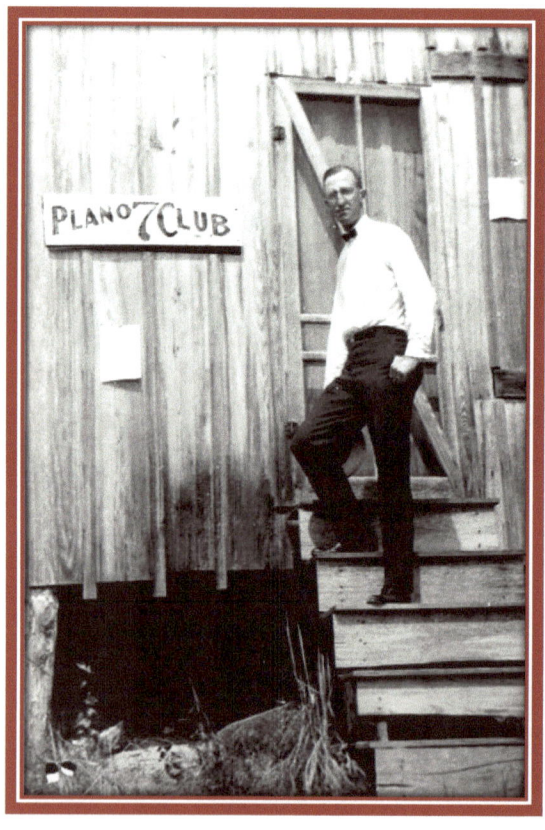

Clowning around

1920s style

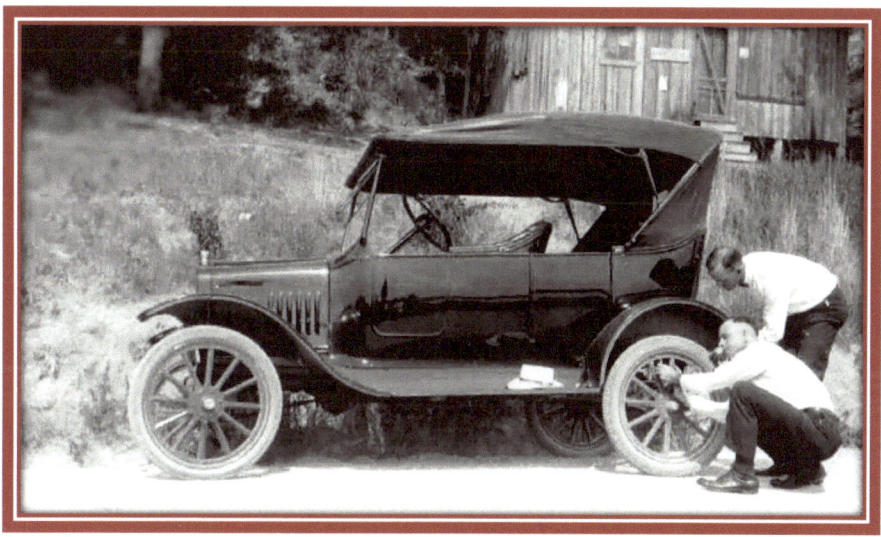

Looks like someone has just purchased a brand new Model T Ford!

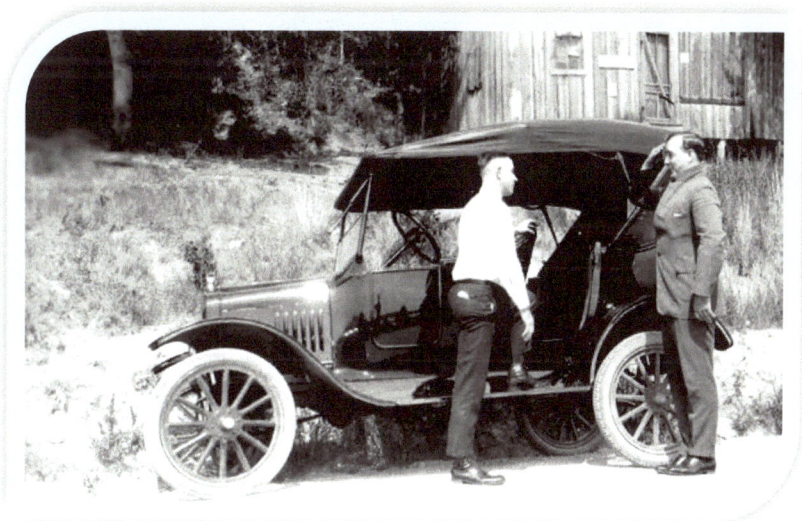

"The Chauffeur"

HUNTING & FISHING

AN ALL-OUT EFFORT

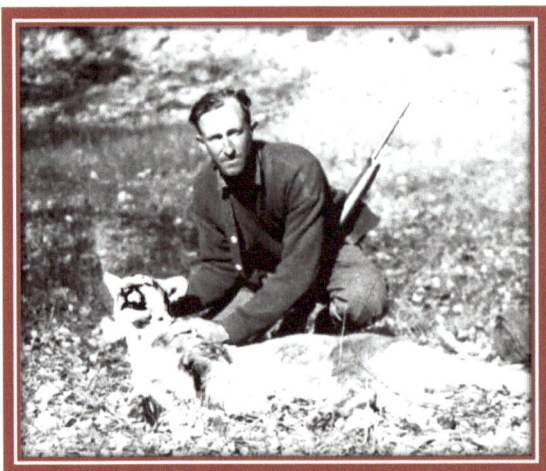

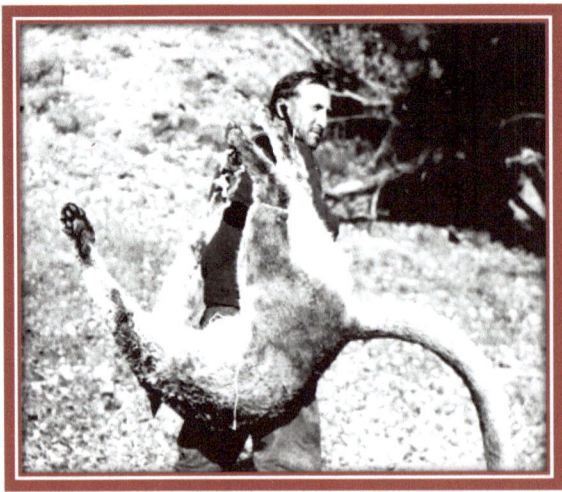

The day Dad bagged a mountain lion

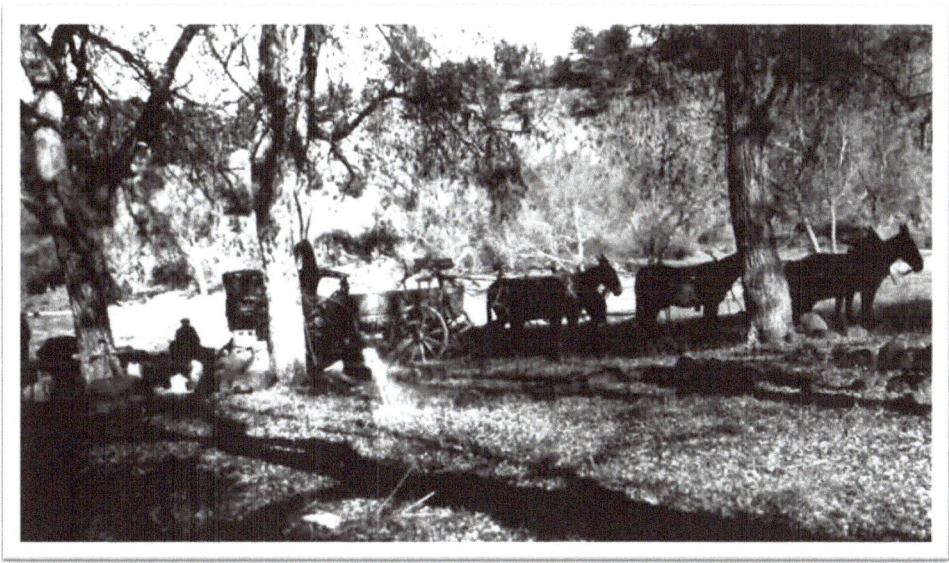

Beginning stage of a serious hunting safari.

The mule train.

Hunting Expedition

(Best photo restoration possible)

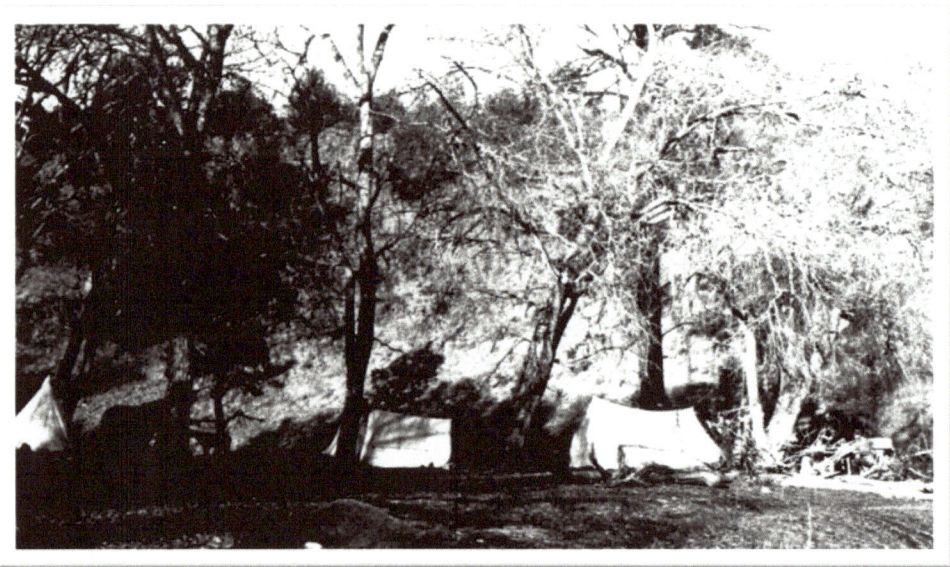

The Campsite

Dad – Off to the hunt

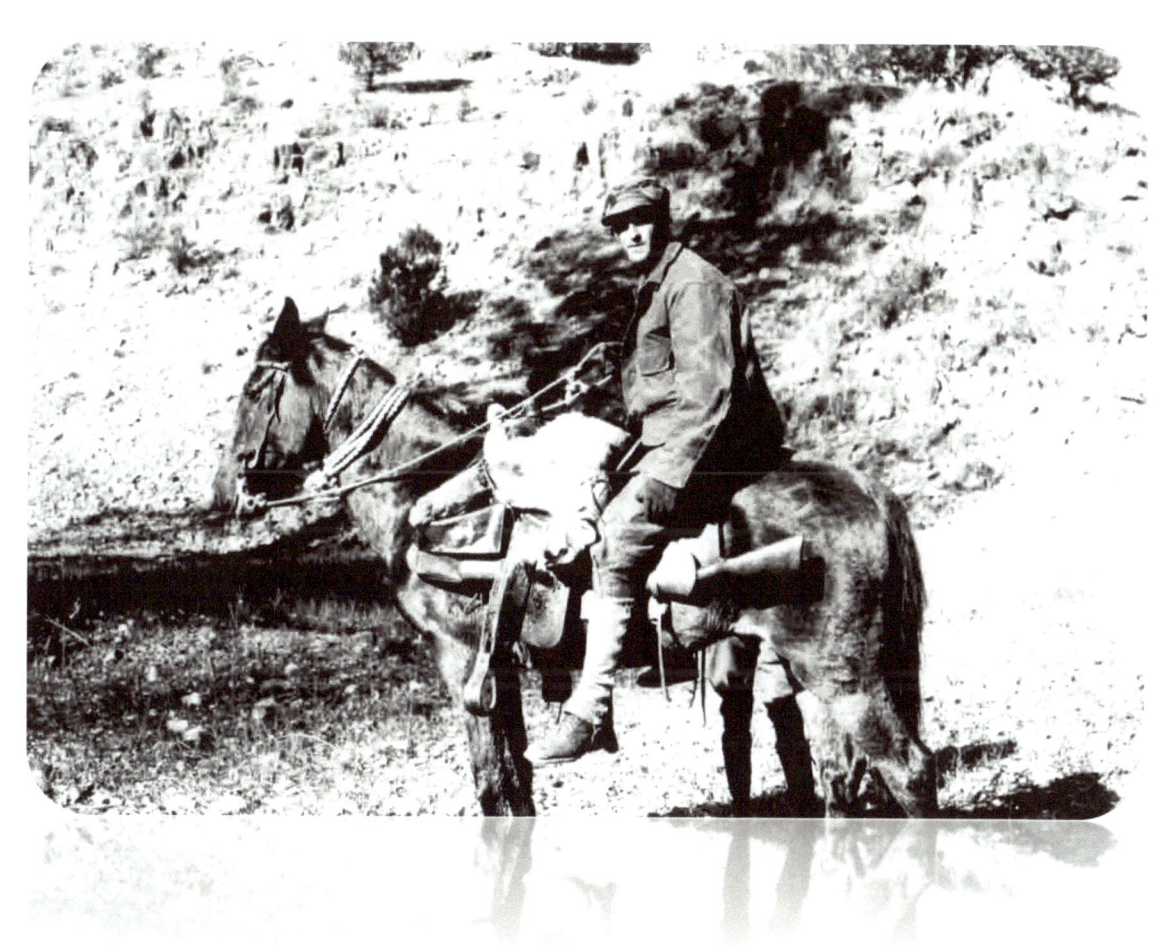

Two deer bagged

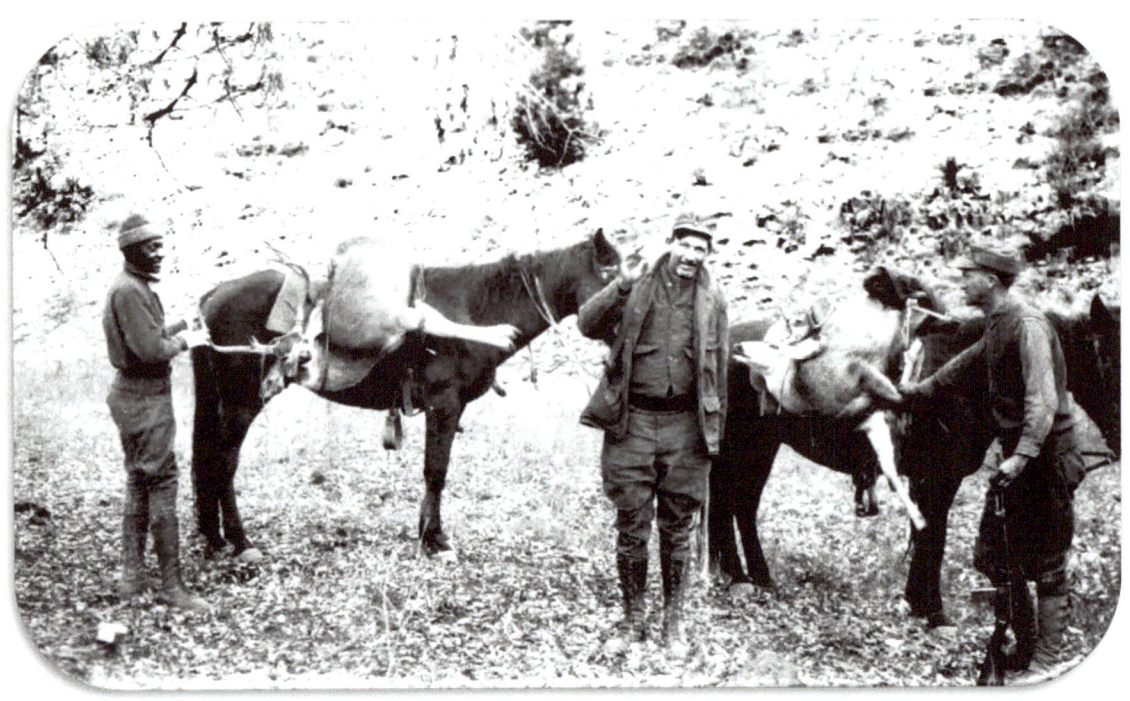

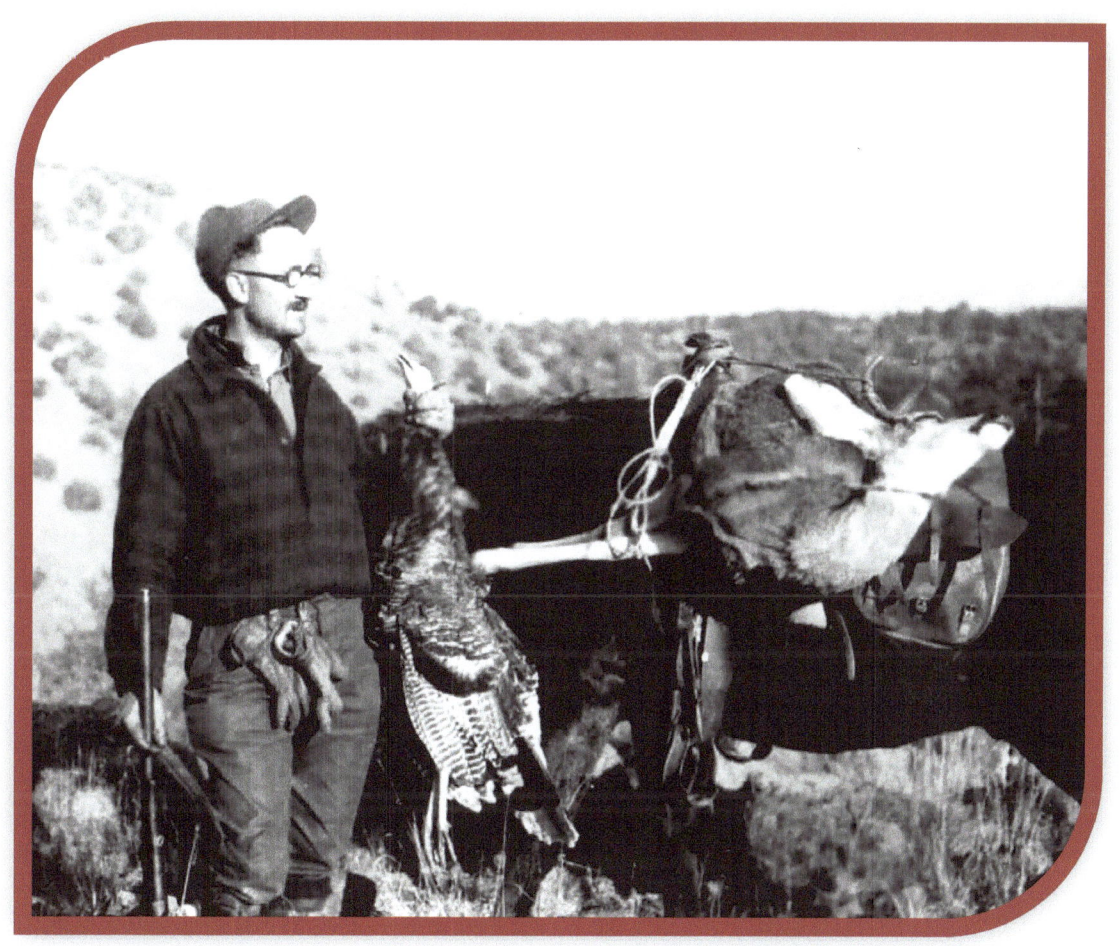

Dad's buddy with his deer - plus a wild turkey.

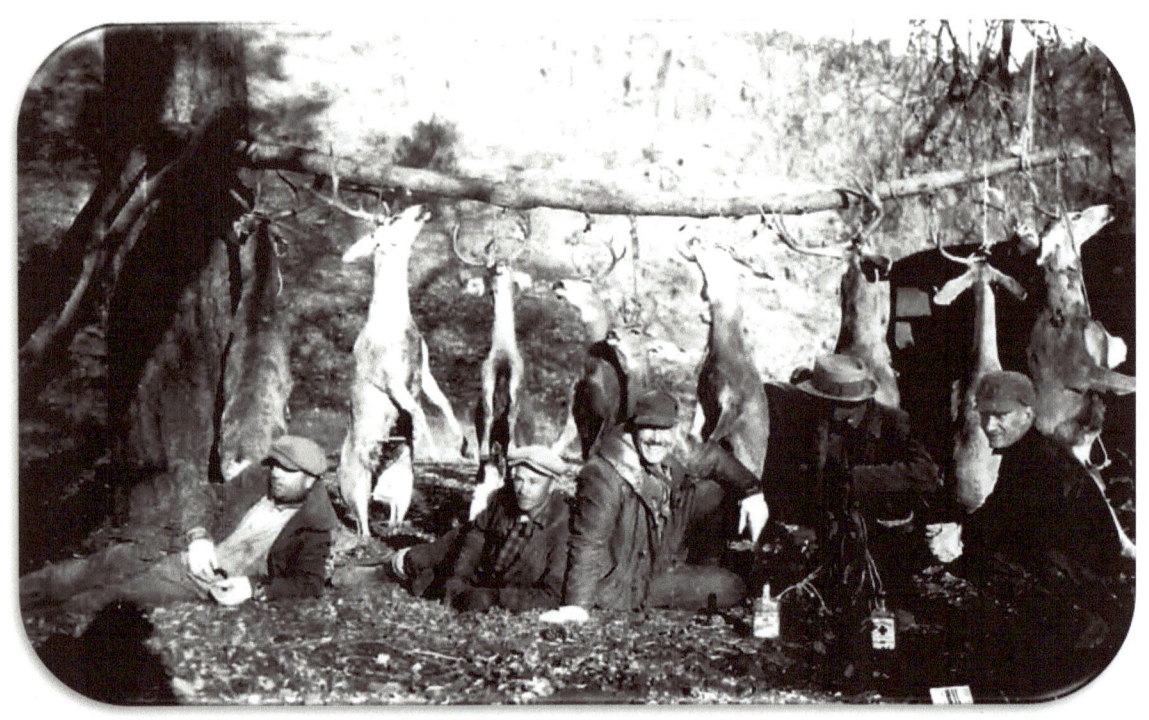

A successful expedition

Six hunters – eight deer

OFF TO MEXICO

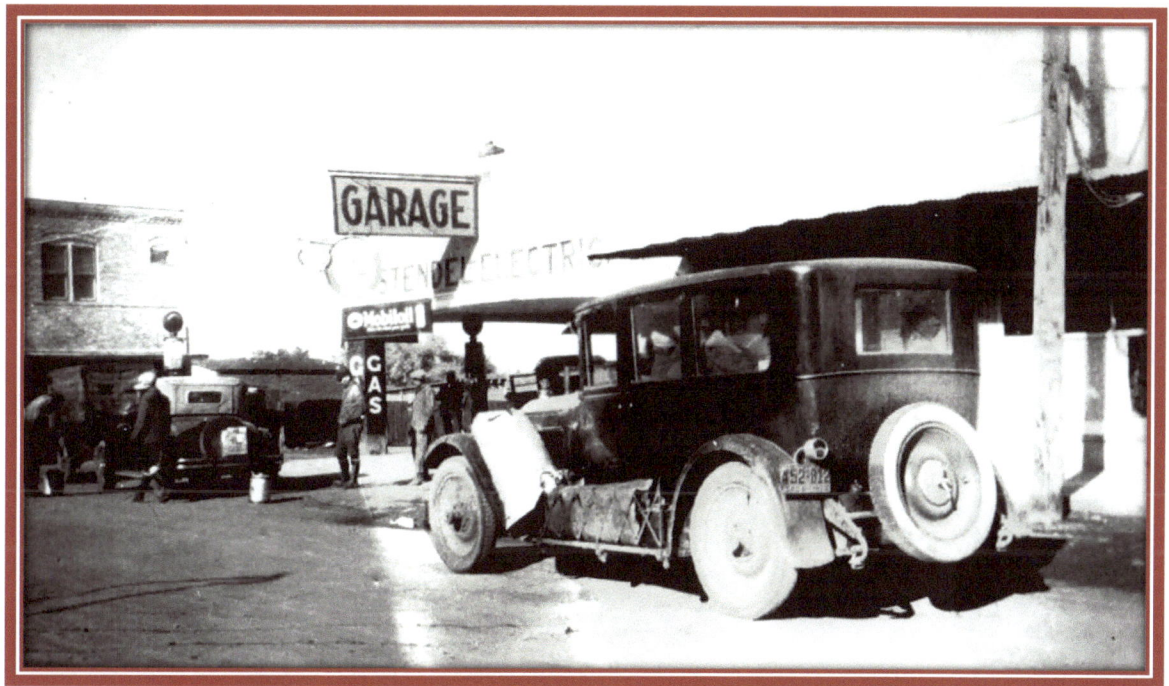

A stop along the way.

Notice the heavy coating of mud on the back tire.

Sign of traveling unpaved roads.

A STOP AT THE MEXICAN BORDER

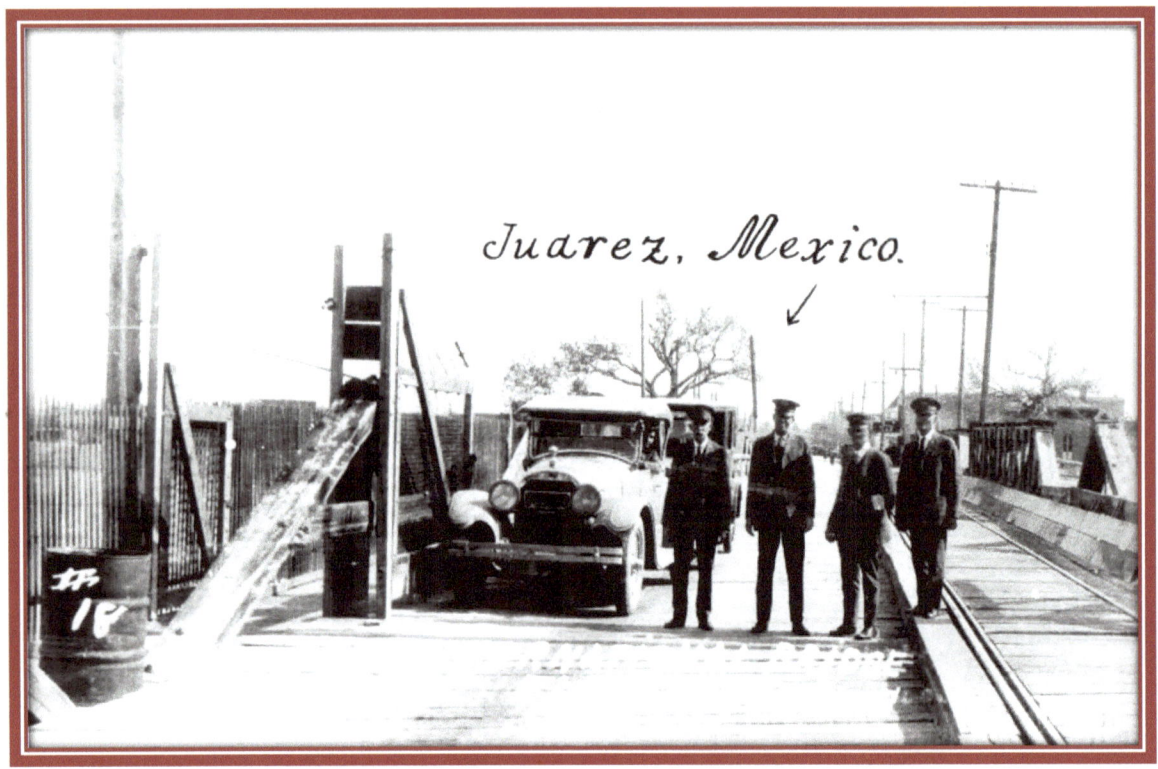

International Bridge – Juarez, Mexico in the background

ANOTHER STOP IN MEXICO

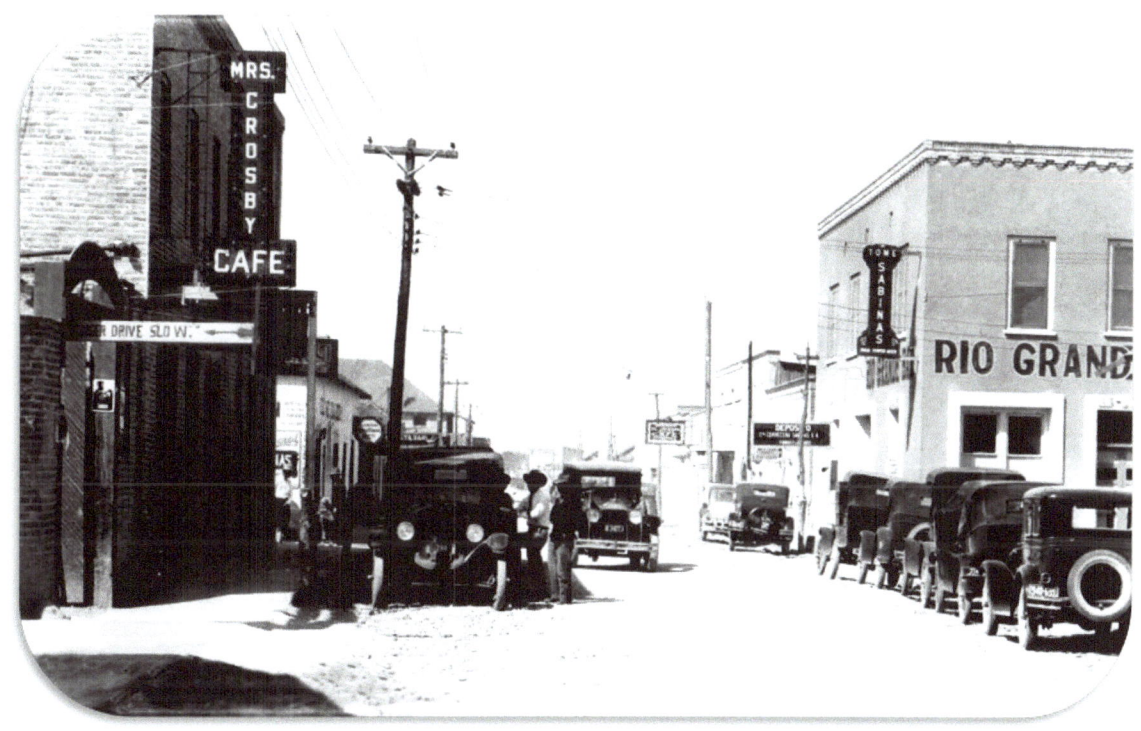

This undated photo was processed in Childress, Texas.

A MEXICAN FAMILY

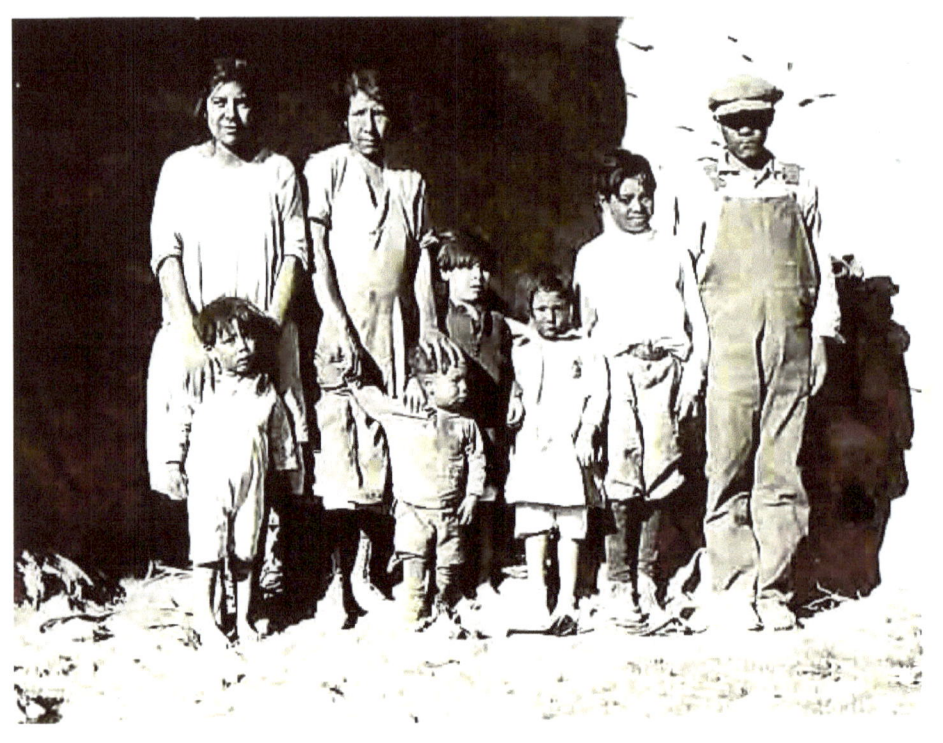

Dad and his buddies were serious duck hunters as well.

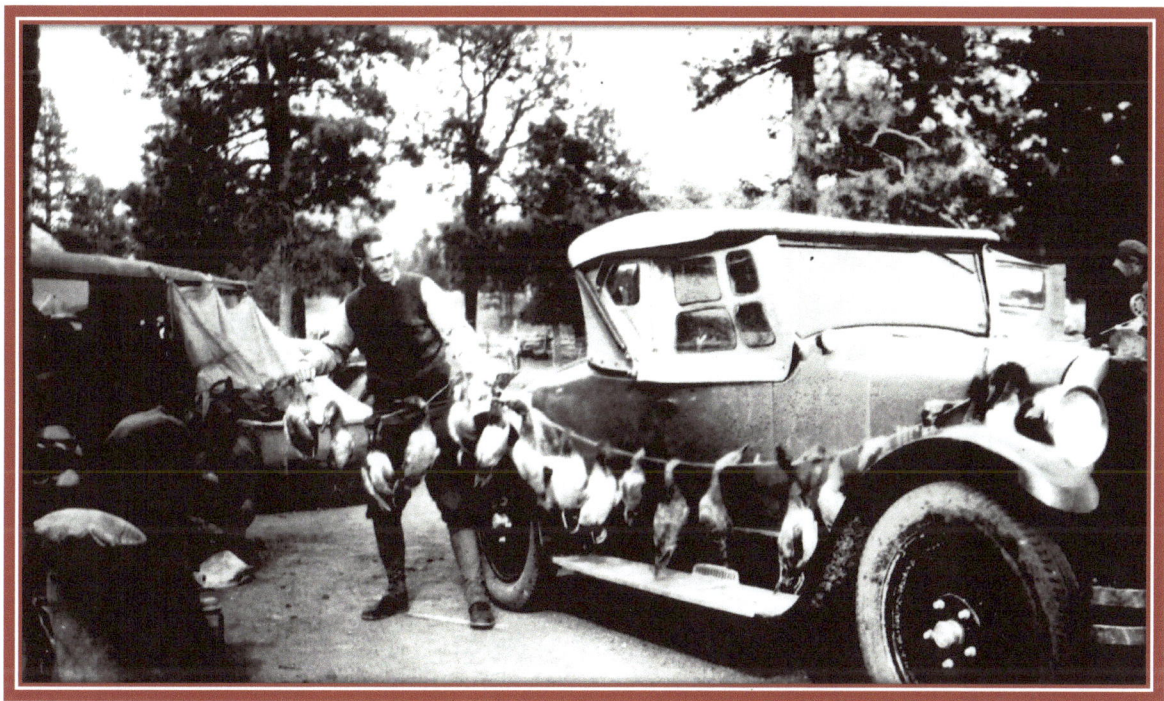

A happy Dad with the expedition's string of ducks.

Hunting was a full-time buddy affair

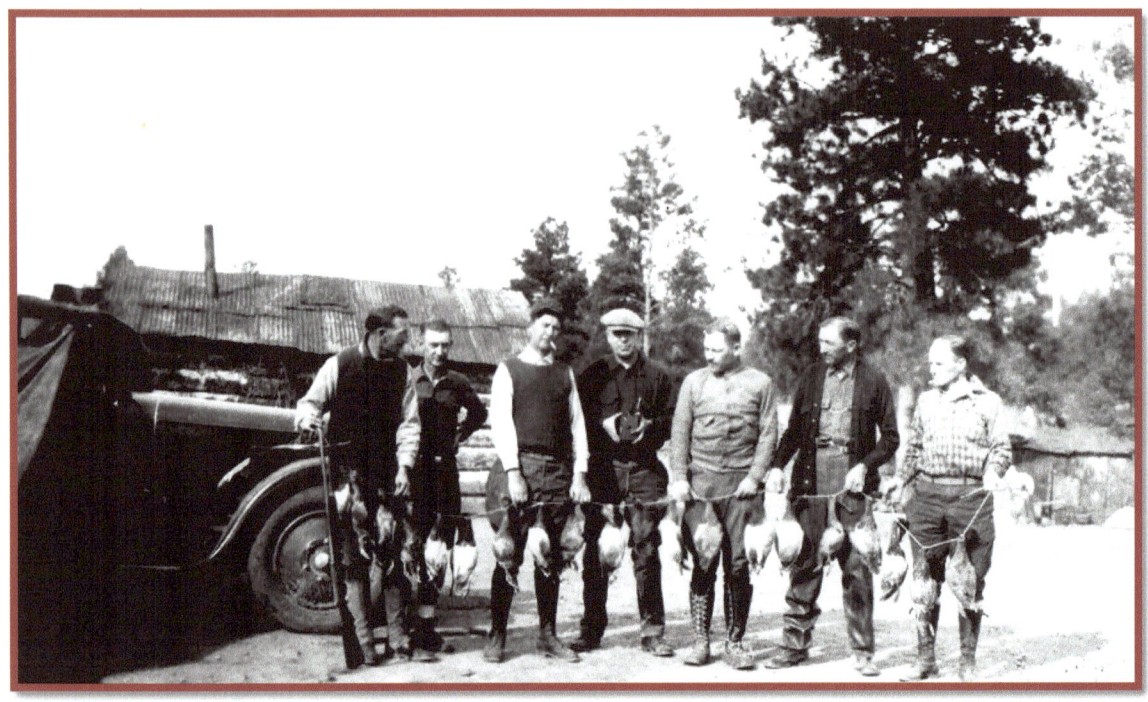

Notice man holding box camera (center)

The ducks at home

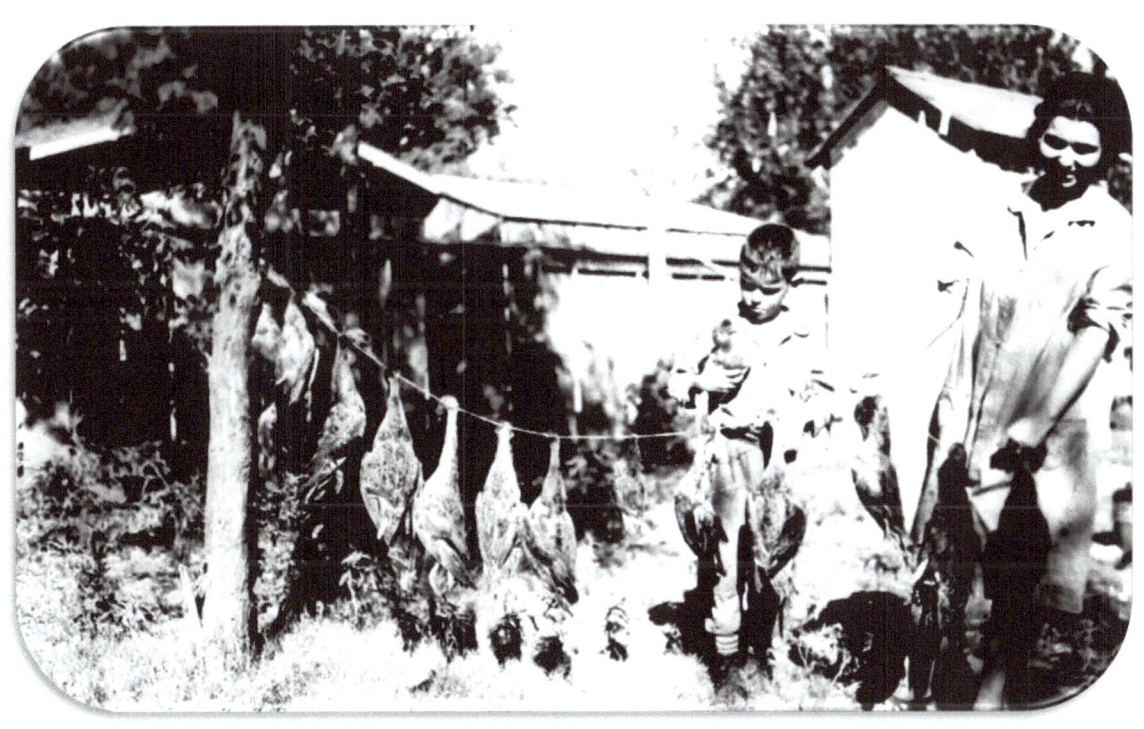

Mom and J. R. with the bounty.

(Best image possible)

Hunting never stopped.

Shooting an armadillo with a pistol.

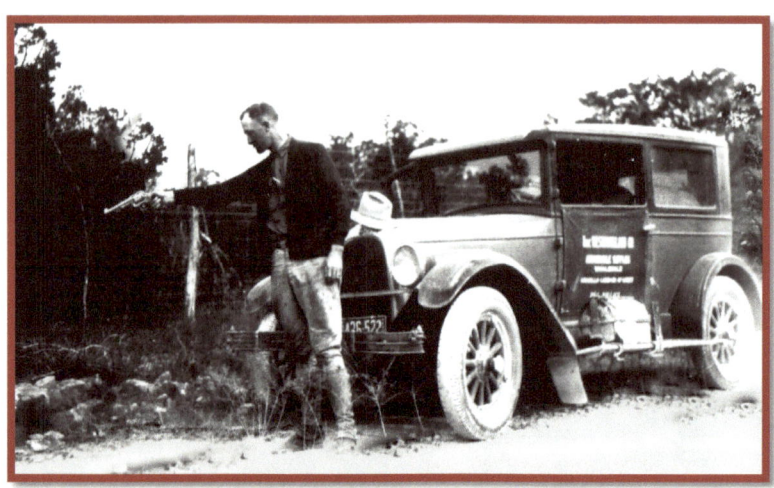

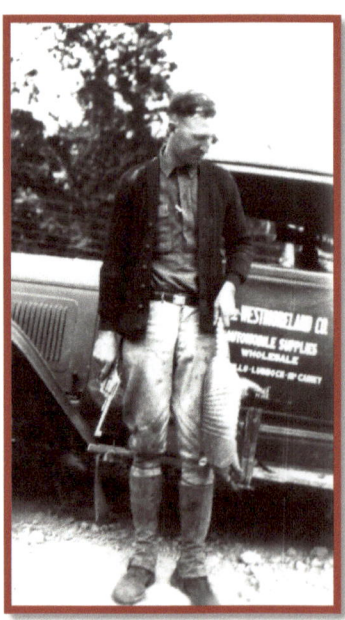

Holding the dead armadillo.

A tame Mountain Lion, photographed somewhere during their hunting escapades

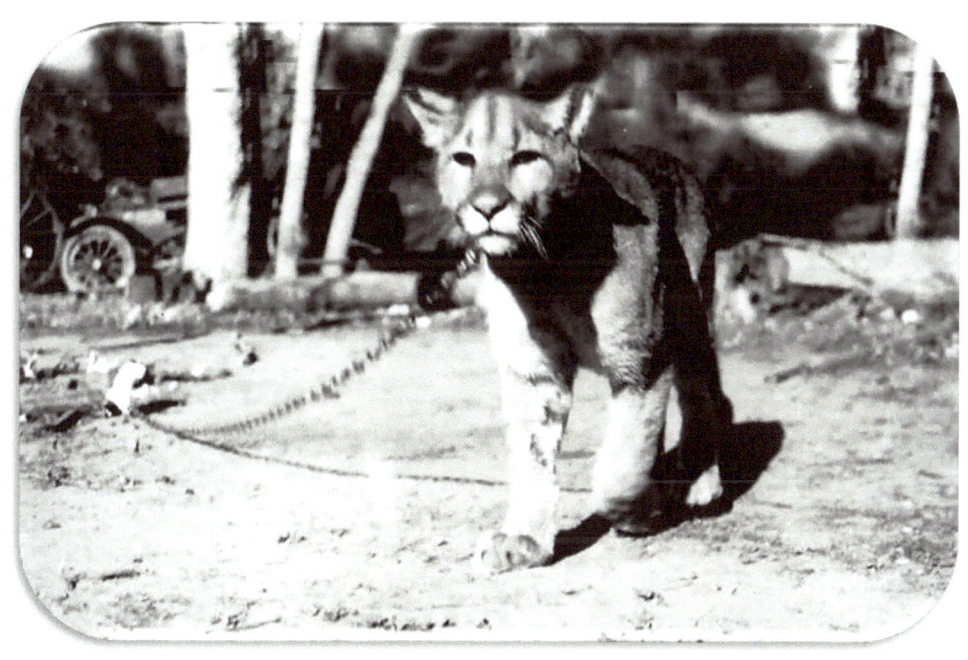

Unfortunately, no background information is available – just amazing photos.

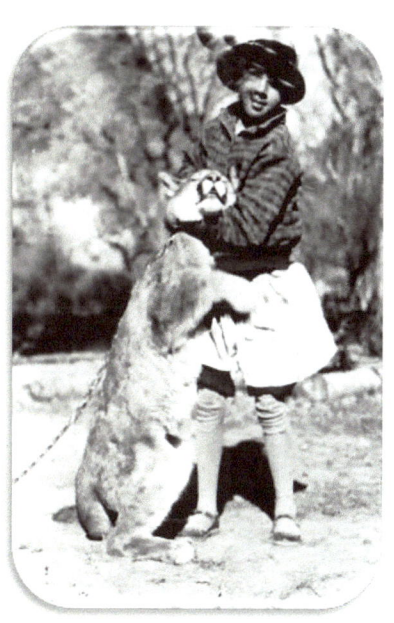

No doubt no-limit fishing

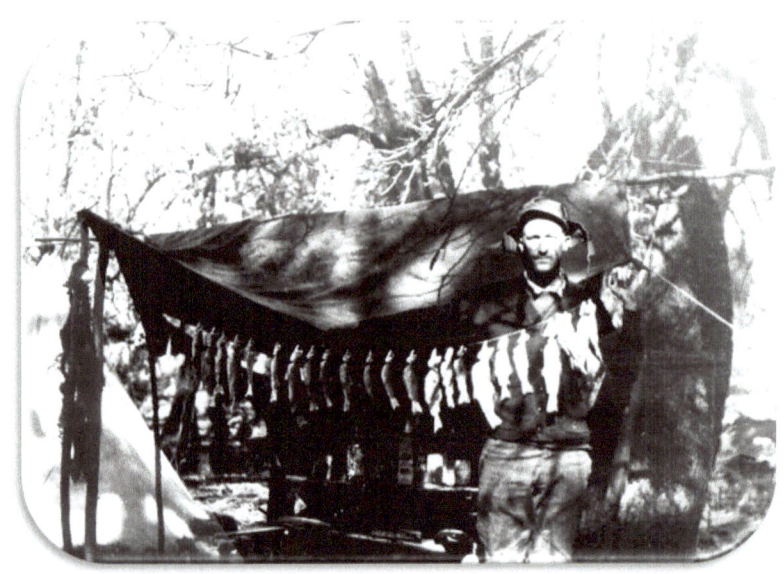

Dad with the day's catch.

This is a camp-shared string.

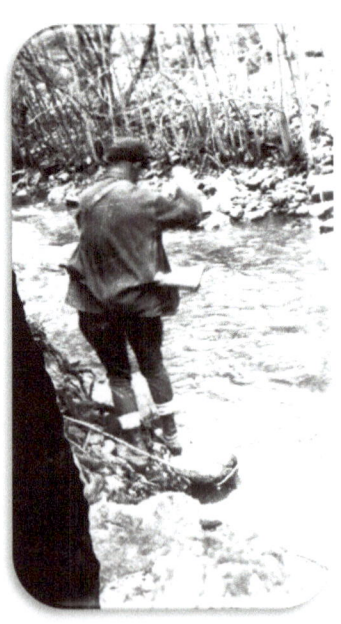

THEIR TRAVELS - FAR AND WIDE

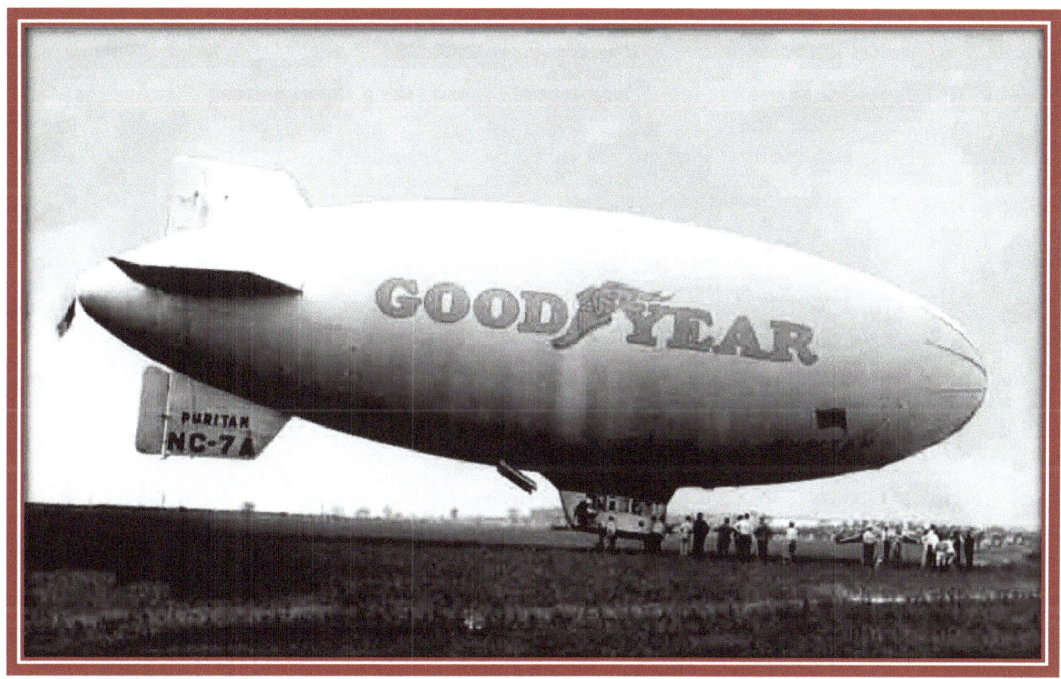

A visit to Notre Dame University
while the Good Year blimp was also visiting.
Dad must have had enough pull to get a ride in the blimp.

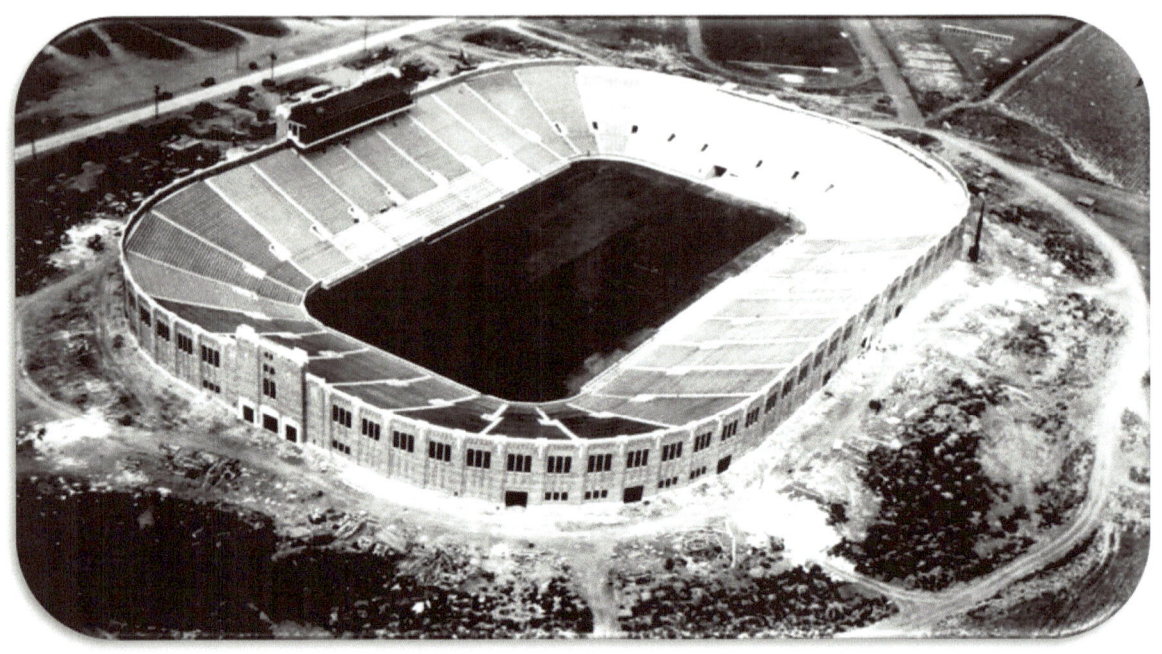

Aerial view - Notre Dame Stadium under construction
(circa 1930)

Another amazing photo

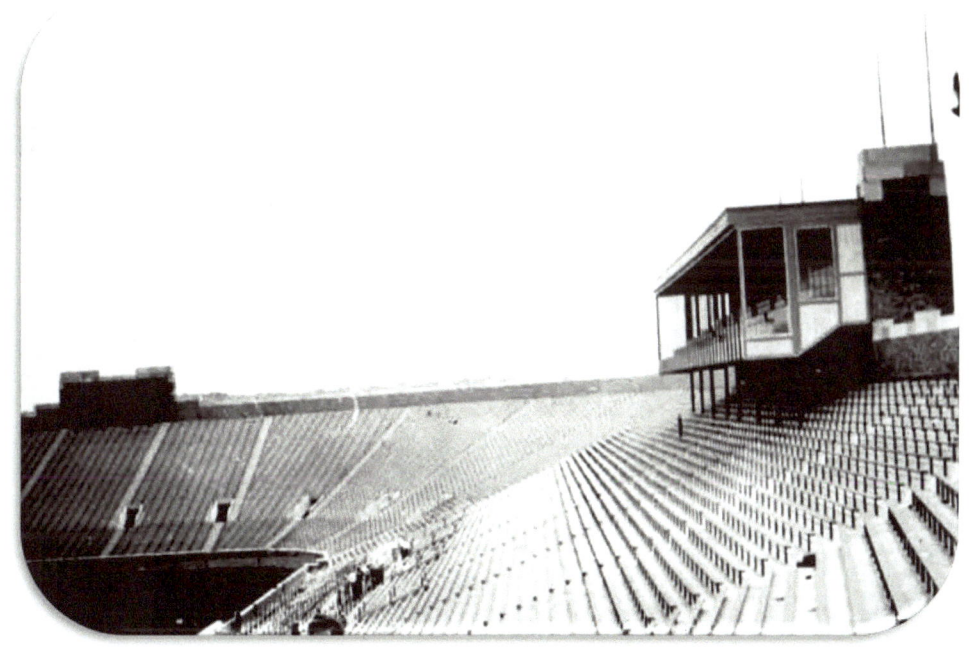

Interior view of the stadium - Much simpler then.

The Notre Dame University Campus – circa 1930

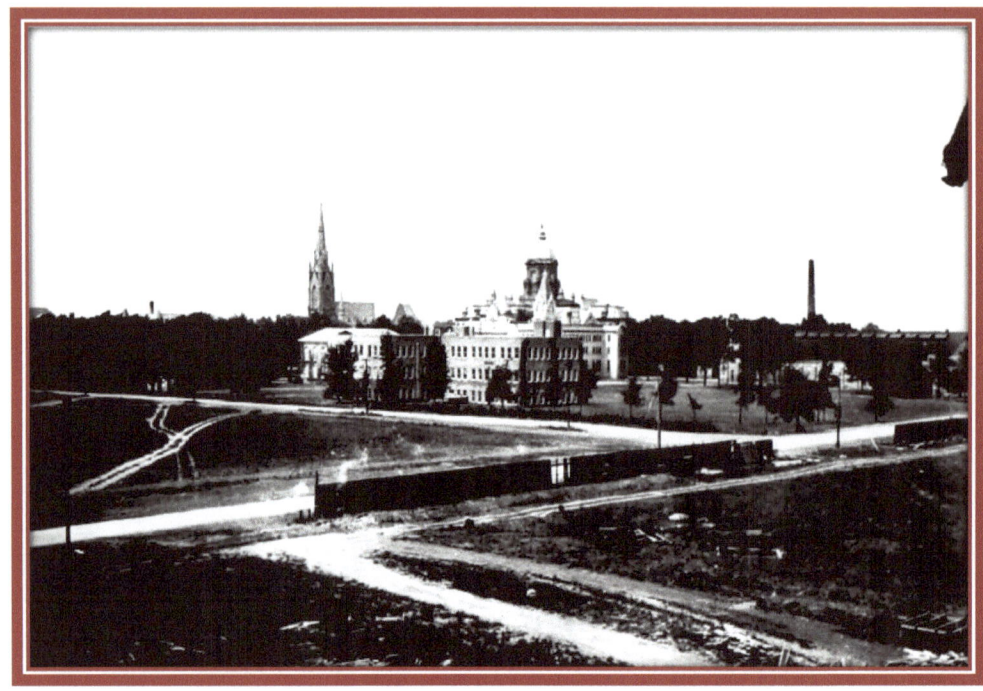

Distant view

Sights along the way

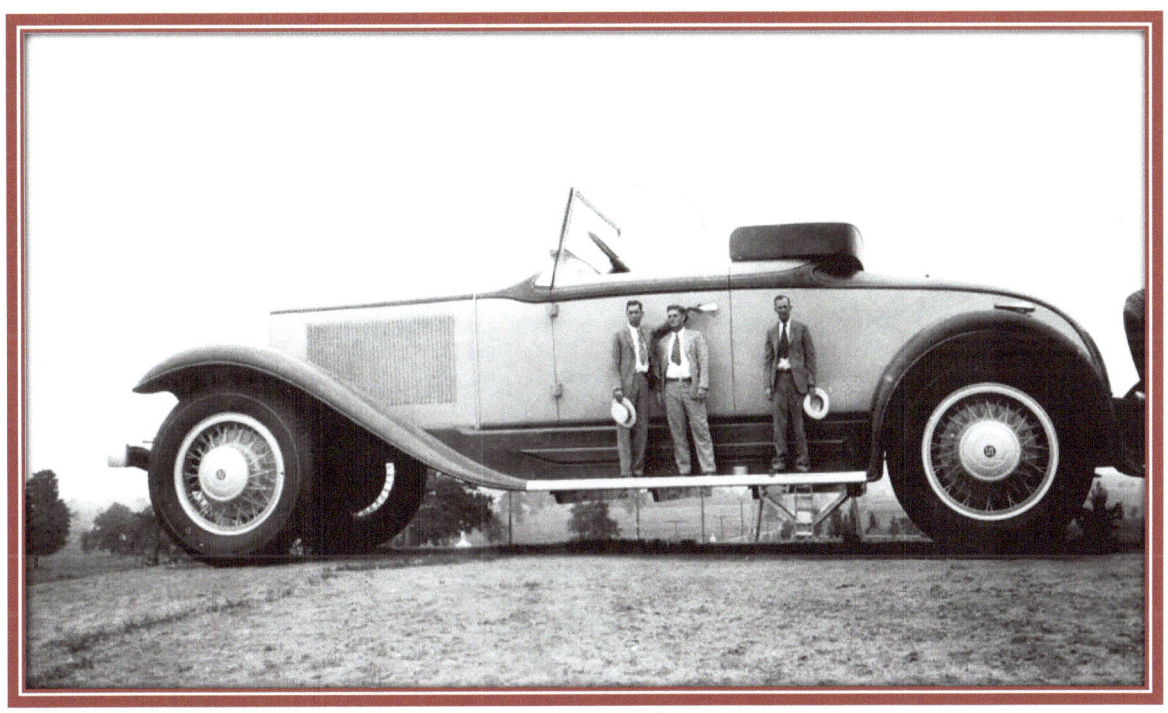

**That's Dad and his buddies on the running board.
Unfortunately, no information is available
on this super-sized car's location**

Teddy Roosevelt encampment – found with album.

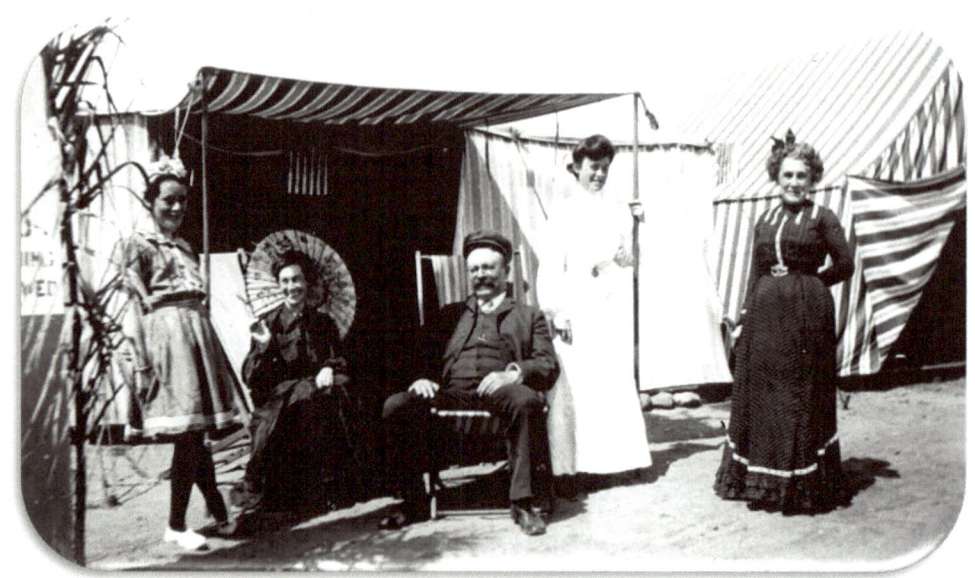

No word regarding the family's possible luck with meeting the President.

A stop at the historic Alamo

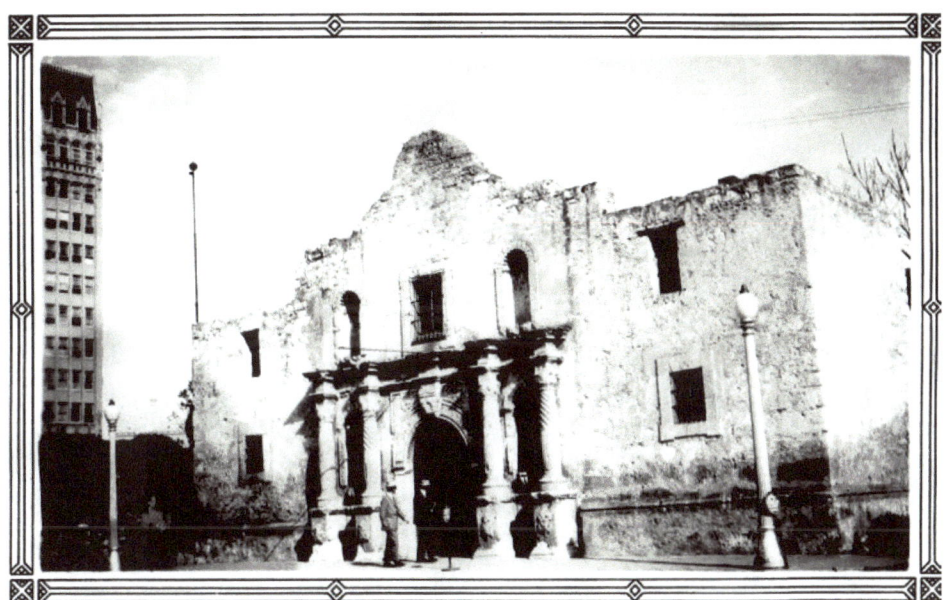

The Alamo
San Antonio, Texas

AN ALBUM OF THE ROARING TWENTIES
Dad made it to the East Coast.

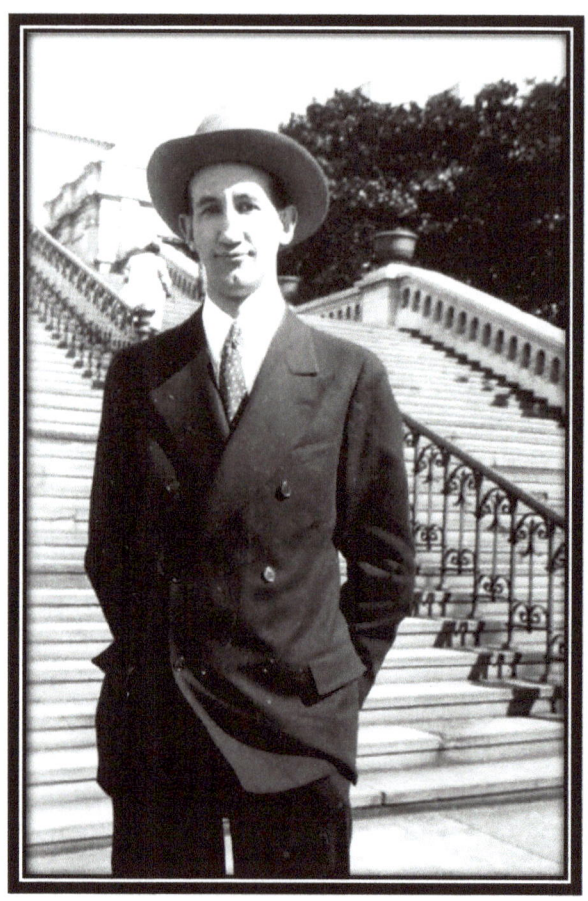

Dad at U.S. Capitol Building

No information about other family members.

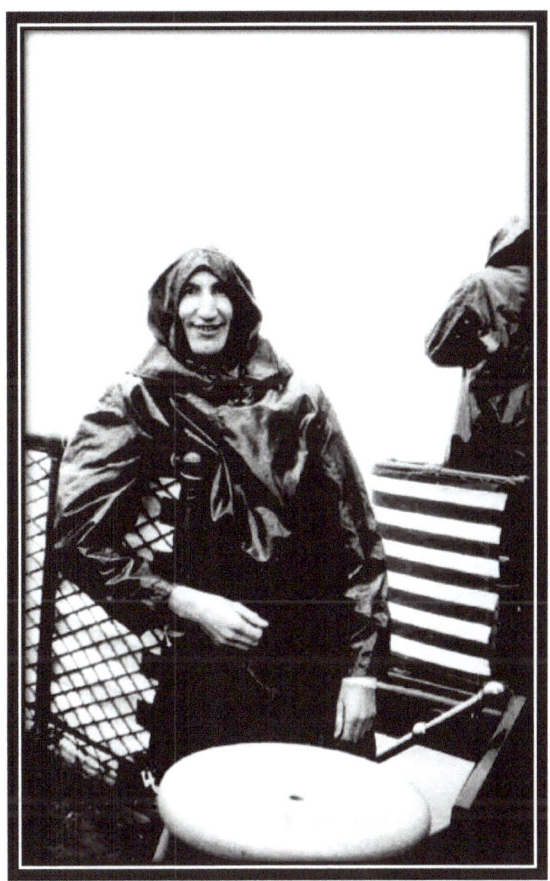

Dad at Niagara Falls
(Maid of the Mist)

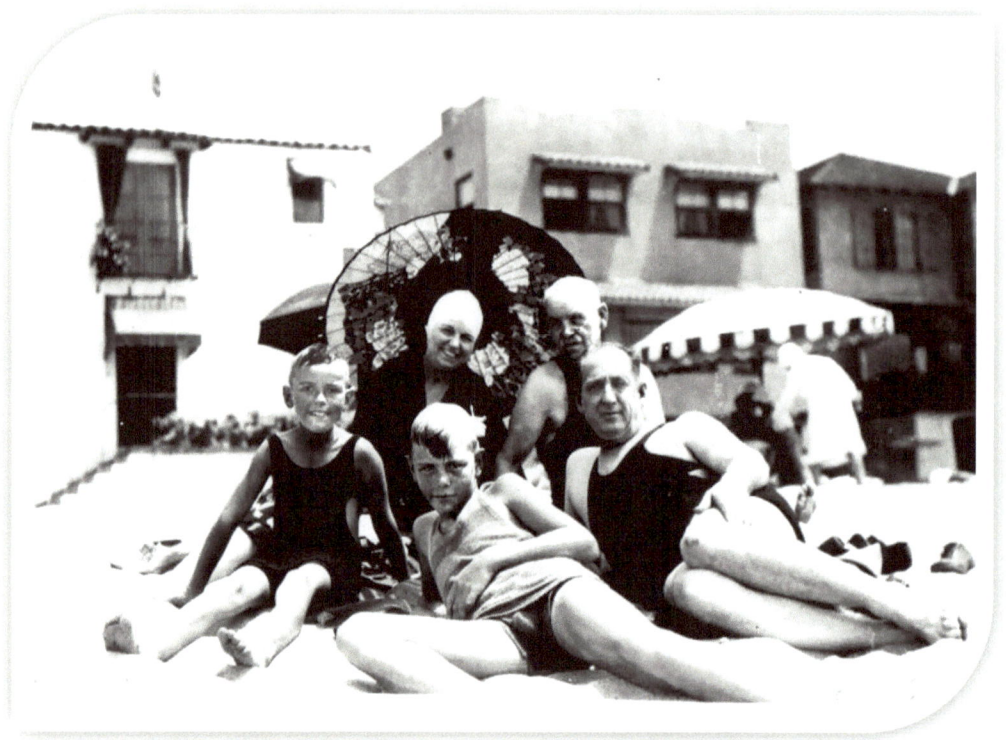

Here they are at the sunny shores of California.

J. R. and Dad enjoying an outing at the local lake.

LIFE ON THE HOME FRONT

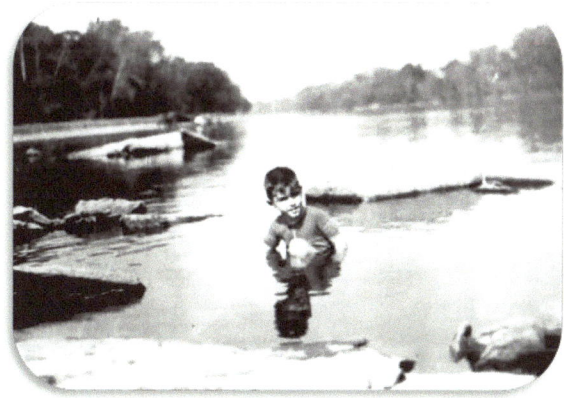

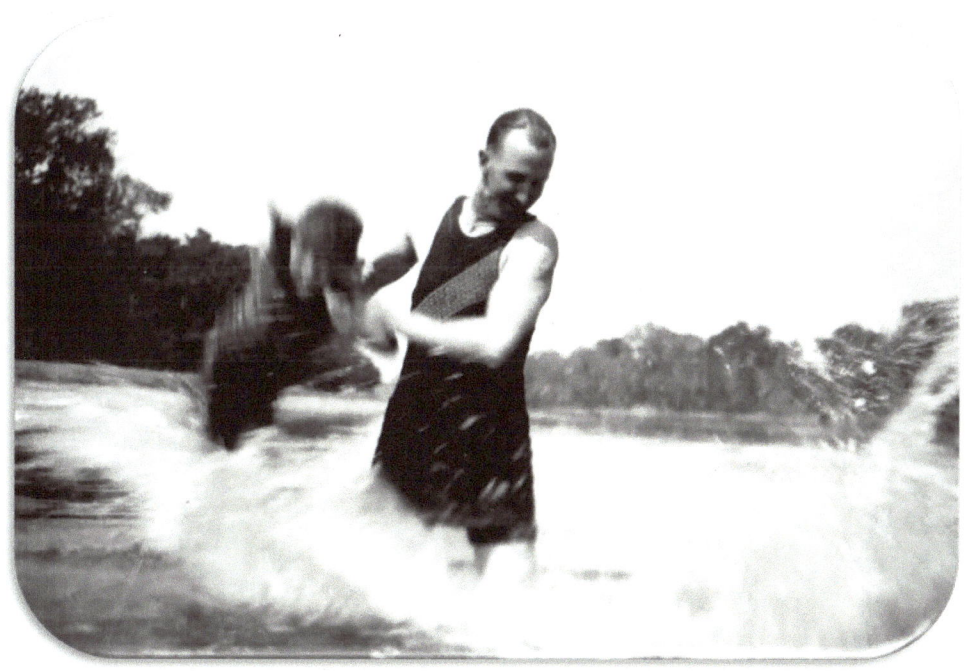

Picnic on the Lakeshore

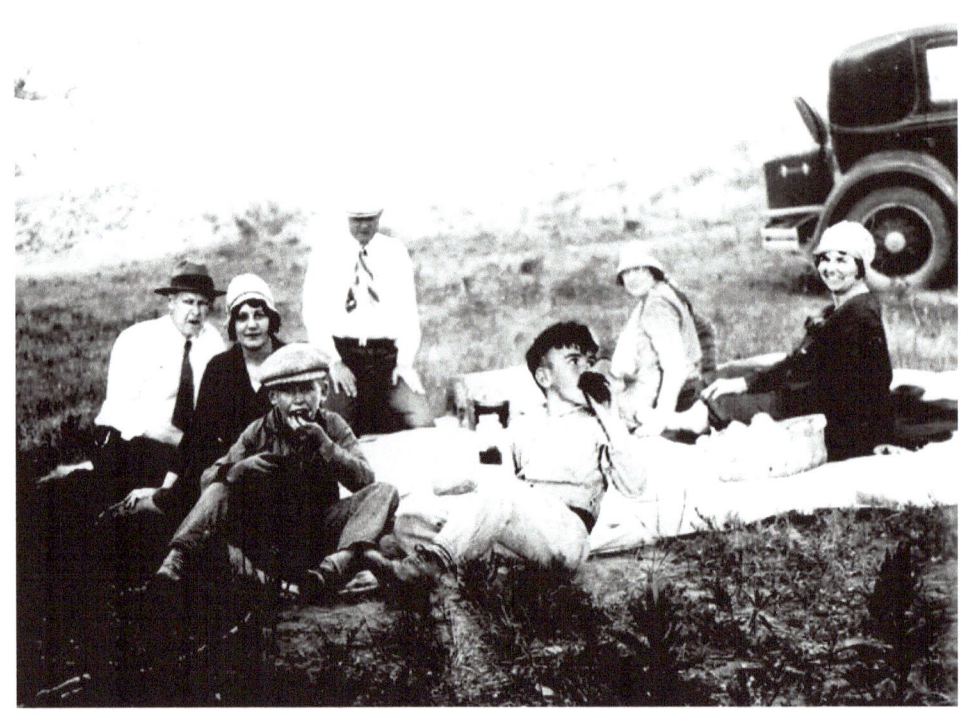

Look at the smile on Mom's face.

Five men in a small boat

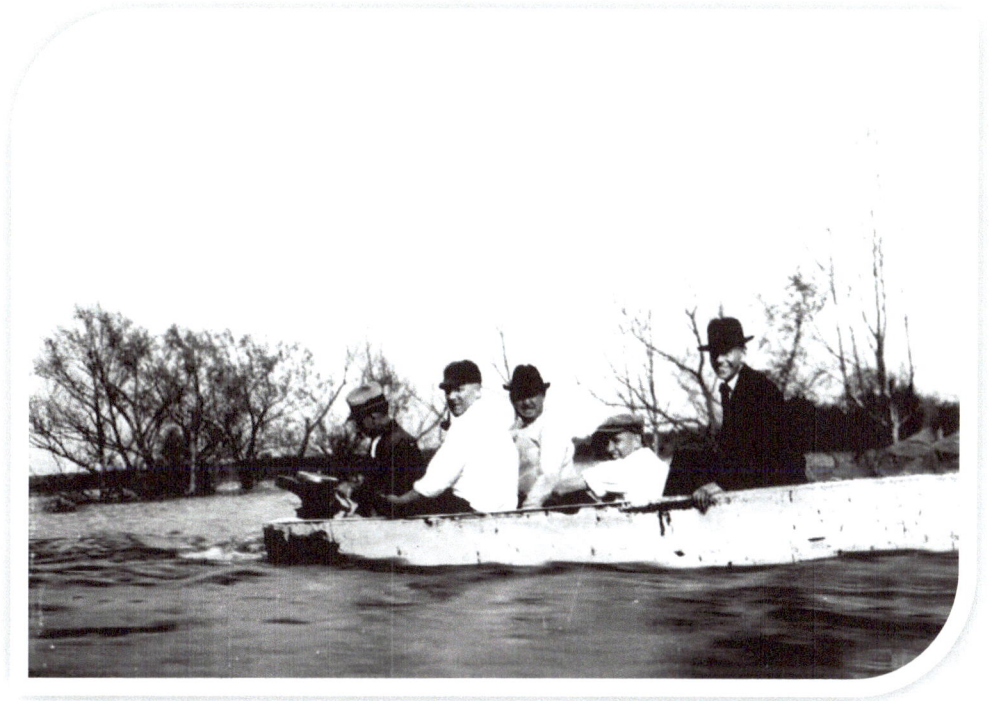

Wow! Couldn't have this many men in a boat under today's safety rules!

AN ALBUM OF THE ROARING TWENTIES

Dad was true and blue Kiwanis Club member.

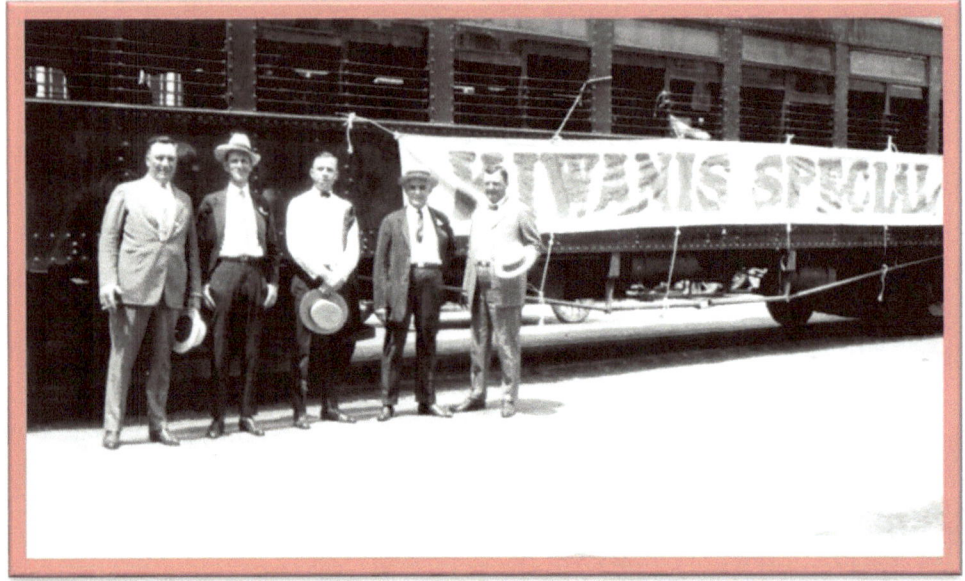

Historic photo of 1920s "Flappers"

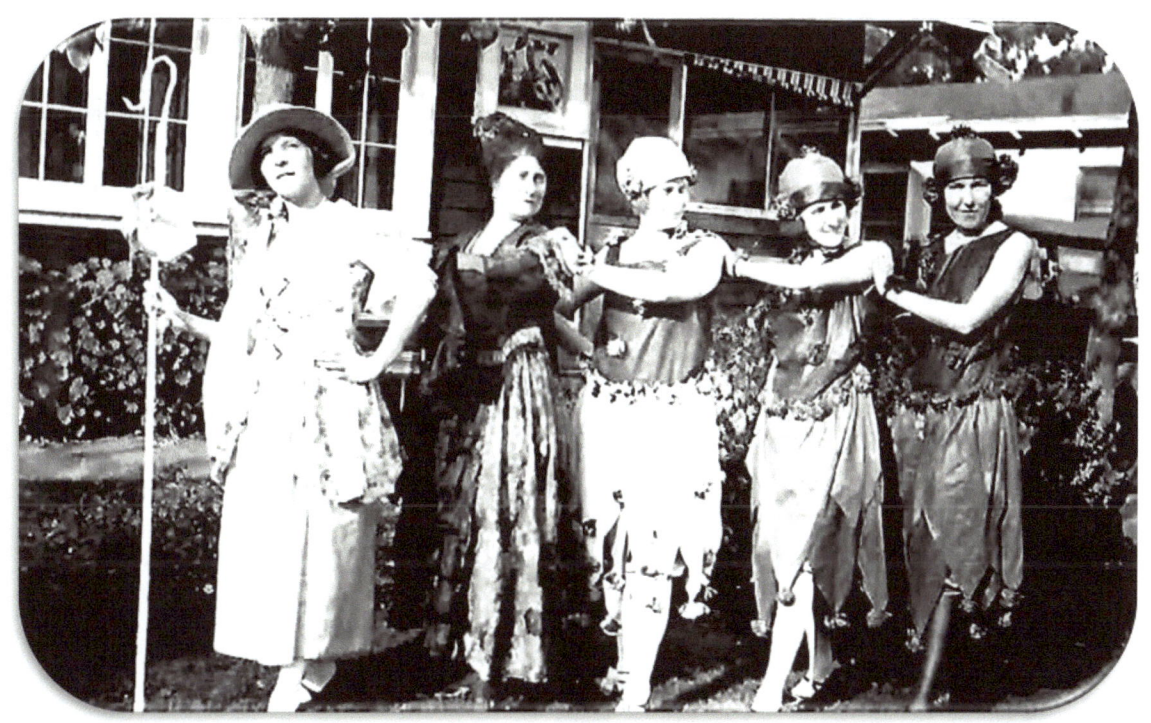

J. R.'s mother at right

Another "Flappers" hi-jinks

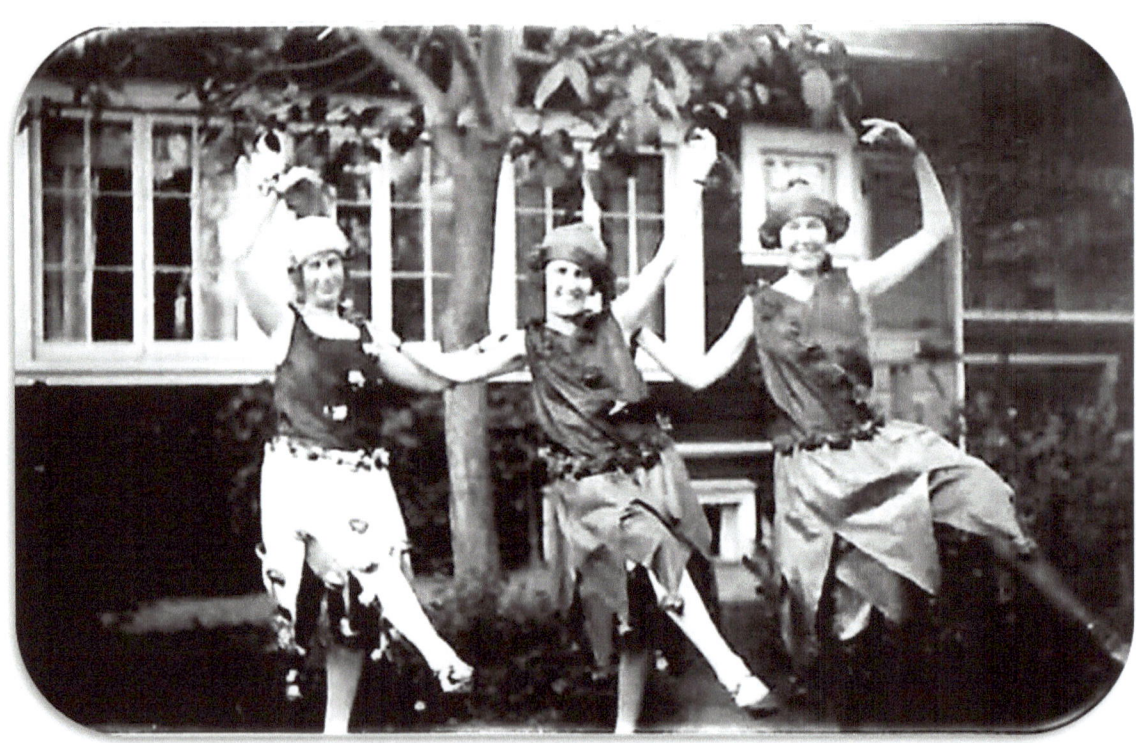

Again, J. R.'s mother at right

Could this be the very beginning of railroading?

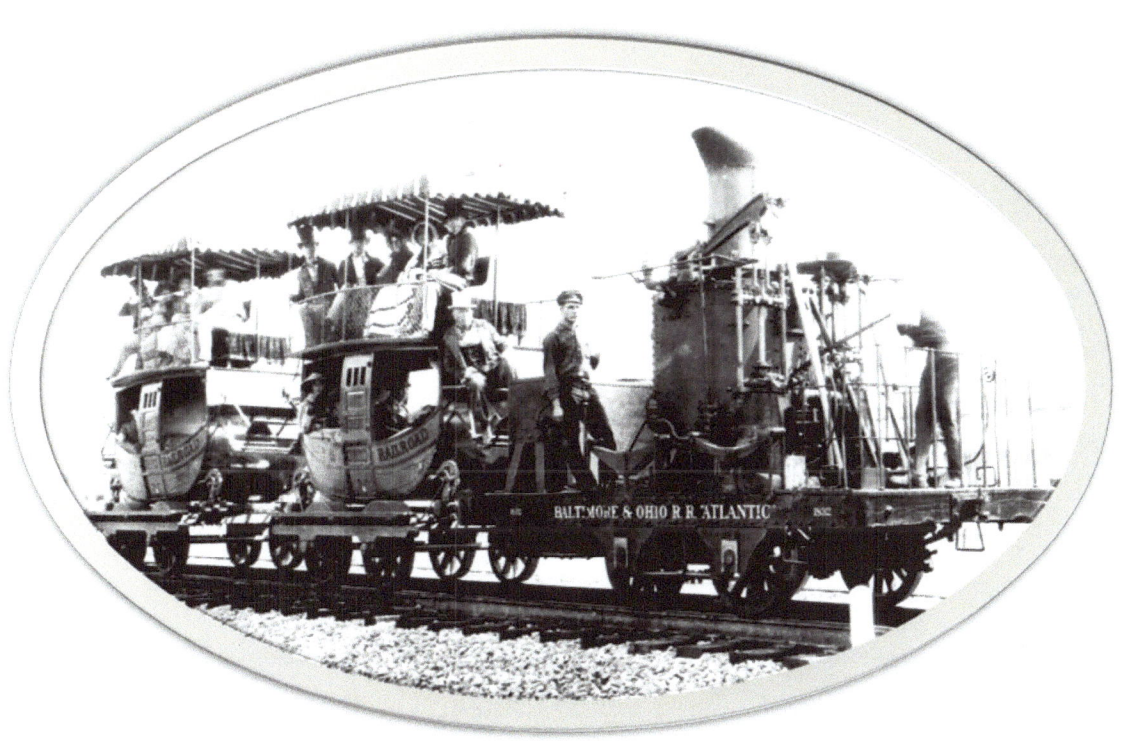

THE END

Clarence Robert Tower is a lifelong resident of California's Silicon Valley. He is self-taught artist but can claim brief contributions to the commercial art profession with book illustrations and artistic contributions to Muscular Dystrophy national campaigns (See drawing below). Mr. Tower spent his professional years as a Civil engineer and Licensed Land Surveyor during the Silicon Valley's growing years. As unusual as it might seem, his profession afforded him major contributions to his art career. Prior to the emergence of computer technology, engineering plans and Official Subdivision Maps were accomplished entirely by hand with old-style pens that were hand loaded with India ink and subsequently applied to starched linen. With that being the case, preparing these maps made up a major portion of an engineer's responsibilities. Engineering firms in those early years were somewhat judged by the artistry of their recorded documents. To keep up with competition, working engineers were compelled to become better than average artists.

After completing his published books, Seventy Years in the Silicon Valley, an Anecdotal History, The Adventures of Zack Gentry, a Tongue and Cheek History of the Opening of the West, a children's book The life of a Teddy Bear Family and an Arcadia Publications book, Legendary Locals of Santa Clara, he realized he had accumulated a huge collection of photos, digital images and image-building information, dating back 59 years, which he could pass on. Included within an assortment of pen-and-ink drawings is a significant number of Santa Clara's historical structures, many of which were visited during the city's Christmas Home Tours.

This drawing was used nationwide by Muscular Dystrophy

www.ingramcontent.com/pod-product-compliance
Lightning Source LLC
Chambersburg PA
CBHW051049180526
45172CB00002B/565

* 9 7 8 1 5 4 5 3 0 5 2 8 7 *